LOCOMOTION PAPERS

RAILWAYS IN THE SIRHOWY VALLEY

by
W.W. Tasker

THE OAKWOOD PRESS

ISBN 0 85361 415 6

First Edition 1978
Second Enlarged Edition 1992

Typeset by Gem Publishing Company, Brightwell, Wallingford, Oxfordshire.

Printed by Alpha Print, Witney, Oxon

A 1922 view of Argoed Village, High Street showing the site of the original Tramroad down the deserted road. It was the only outlet for Cwm Creeich Colliery until the 1910 period when a siding was put in near the colliery screens. *Author's Collection*

Front cover.
A special saddle tank No. 88 seen here at Sirhowy station in the 1880s. This locomotive was built at Crewe in 1875 (Works No. 1956); duplicate list No. 3152; LMS No. 7328, and finally scrapped in May 1927. *Courtesy D. Bowen*

Published by
The OAKWOOD PRESS
P.O.Box 122, Headington, Oxford.

Contents

A view looking from the down platform at Sirhowy station in the early LNWR days.
Lens of Sutton

GENTLEMEN
BOOKING OFFICE AND WAITING ROOM

Introduction

My father spent his entire working life on the Merthyr, Tredegar and Abergavenny section of the LNW Railway, except for a short spell in the Manchester area, and travelled to all parts, including sections of the Abergavenny–Merthyr line, from our house at Argoed. If you can imagine it, this entailed, before public road transport came, getting to places on foot and covering quite considerable distances over the week.

The history of the Sirhowy Tramroad and the Sirhowy Railway Company have, of course, been covered before, but my main interest was the LNWR, LMS and BR period – one which I grew up with, and I got to know many of the staff during my journeys to Newport from 1927 to 1931. I knew most of the drivers. I recall one occasion when I spent two hours at Risca station; the 9.05 pm passenger ex-Newport was delayed because of a derailment at Brickworks Siding between Risca and Nine Mile Point. It was a cold winter's night, with the frost glistening, and it was not long before the driver came along and said 'Would you like a warm in the cab?'. Needless to say, I wasn't long taking advantage of that suggestion!

Valuable assistance has come from Mr C.H. Forrester, son of the late Mr Henry Forrester, former station master at Blackwood in 'North Western' days; but the main purpose of this revision is the discovery and inclusion of many early unpublished photographs of the Tredegar area by Mr Gerald Davies and a new selection of photographs of the Pontllanfraith district including the Valley's Collieries by Mr Wayne Hopkins. Additional information on Hall's Road is from Mr Malcolm James and Mr R.H. Marrows, with additional material also supplied by Tony Cooke. I have to thank also the many friends who have helped to make this revision worthwhile.

W.W. Tasker
Caldicot, Gwent

A view of Blackwood High Street, looking towards Argoed. The Royal Oak Inn on the right is where the inquests were held on the deaths of workers at local collieries and the tramroad. *Author's Collection*

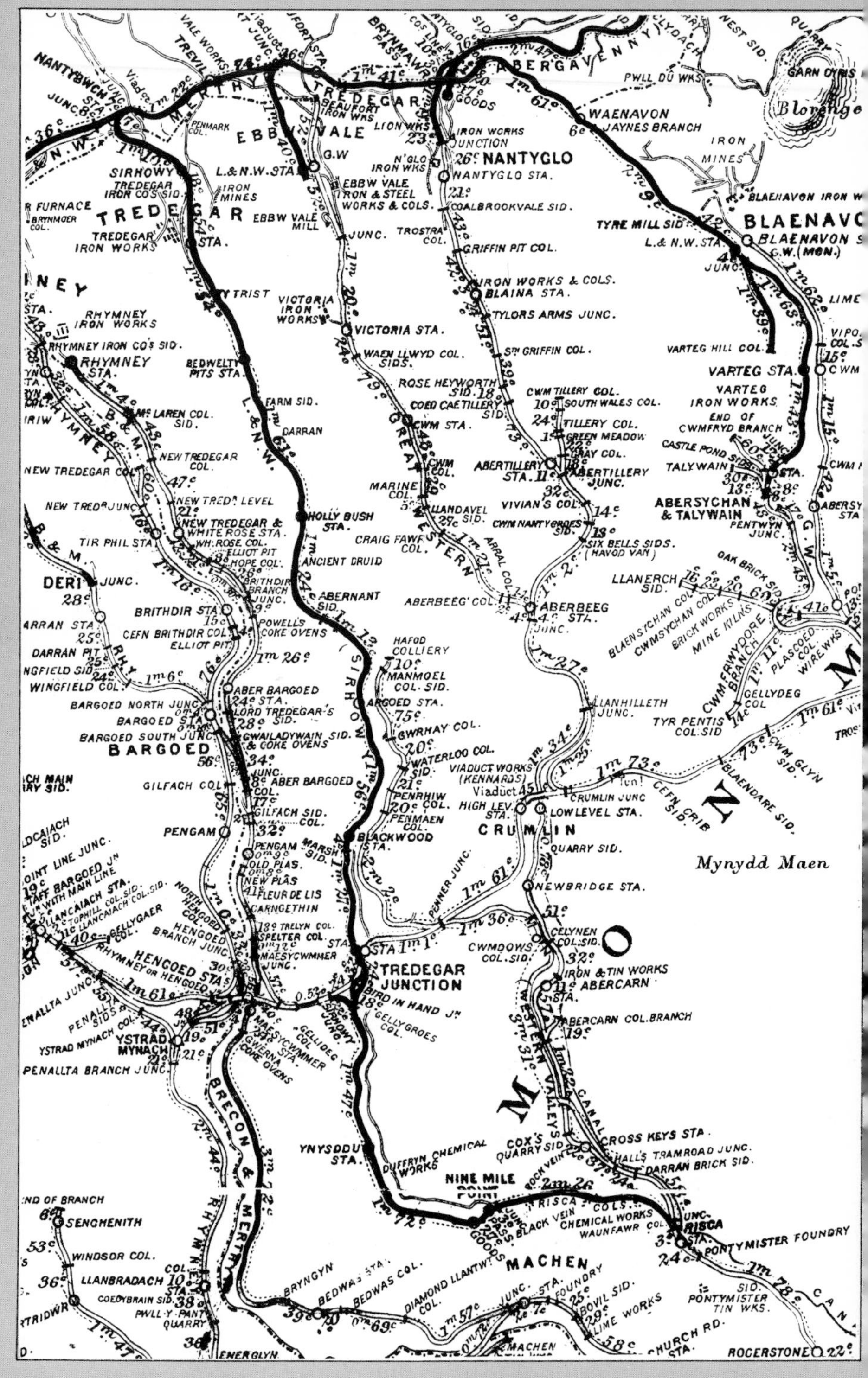

An RCH map of 1921 of the Sirhowy Valley and associated railways.

Chapter One

The Tramroad is Built

Before the coming of the ironworks and collieries, the Sirhowy Valley was wild and untouched by industrial activity. Tredegar was a very small place, and the villages of Argoed and Blackwood were developed after the completion of the Sirhowy Tramroad in approximately 1805. The corn mills at Cwm Corrwg and Gelligroes, together with cottages at Gwrhay were in existence much earlier than either Argoed or Blackwood. The mills utilised the Sirhowy River as a means of power. Records reveal that the Meredith family (*see page 14*) were at Gwrhay in the 15th century, moving later to a house at Argoed named Pwllypant. The rest was isolated small farms and white-washed cottages. There was an extensive woodland area from Argoed to the junction of the Sirhowy and Western Valleys near Risca.

The Sirhowy Tramroad passed through the parishes of Bedwellty and Mynyddislwyn, and the only roads in 1800 were those going across the Valley from east to west, except perhaps the mountain road from the Penllwyn, passing Bedwellty church to a point near Cefn Golau at Tredegar.

Dr William Joseph Davies, a well known surgeon in the Gwent of his day, and at one time living at Penar House near Pontllanfraith, often spoke of his father's transport activities in the early days, when mule trains of iron would come from Dowlais and Merthyr to the coast. If they were making for Newport, their route was down the 'Sunken Lane' past the old Penllwyn Manor House and into the Sirhowy Valley at Gelligroes. From this point forward they followed roughly what was later to be the track of the Llanarth and Penllwyn Tramroad, keeping close to the river for most of the way. Writers referring to Monmouthshire's past can hardly fail to mention Archdeacon Coxe. This is what he had to say when he visited the Sirhowy Valley in the years 1798–99:

> We mounted our horses and travelled along the vale and crossed the Ebwy near the influx of the Sorwy over Pont-y-cymmer. Soon after we ascended the side of the hill, which bounds the vale, and travelled along, through thickets, cornfields and meadows, sprinkled with Hamlets, watered by numerous torrents and overlooking the Sorwy. The featchers of the vale are more wild and romantic than those of the Ebwy – It is deeper and narrower.

He was, of course, referring to the lower part of the Valley, and gives a vivid picture of the unspoiled countryside.

Nicholson's *Cambrian Travellers Guide*, published in 1840, refers to Tredegar's Iron Industry as follows:

> At Tredegar five Furnaces are in operation, all blown with cold air. The Tredegar Iron Co. are building two others, and contemplating building two more, making nine altogether. They now produce 400 to 450 Tons of Cast Iron weekly which is made into Bars, Rails, and Rods.

When the furnaces and coal levels were first started in the Sirhowy Valley district, it soon became apparent that in order to sell the product, it had to be conveyed to the coast; and in this instance, it was to the wharves on the River Usk at Newport.

NOTICE IS HEREBY GIVEN, That application is intended to be made to Parliament in the ensuing Session, for leave to bring in a Bill to amend or repeal the powers and provisions, or some of the powers and provisions of the Local and Personal Act, 42, George 3, chapter 115, incorporating the Sirhowy Tramroad Company, to change their name, and to confer upon them new and altered powers, and to enable them to make and maintain the works or some of the works, with all requisite conveniences connected therewith, and to effect the objects following, or some of them, (that is to say),

No. 1 —The diversion of the parish road from Machen to Mynyddyslwyn, at or near the Ten Mile-post from Newport, on the Sirhowy Tramroad, and in the parish of Machen, and county of Monmouth, so as to carry the same under the Sirhowy Tramroad.

No. 2.—A Deviation Line of Railway, commencing by a junction with the Sirhowy Tramroad, at or near the Eleven Mile-post from Newport, on the Sirhowy Tramroad, in the parish of Machen, in the county of Monmouth, and terminating by a junction with the Sirhowy Tramroad, at or near the Twelve-and-Three-quarter Mile-post on the said Sirhowy Tramroad, in the parish of Mynyddyslwyn, in the same county.

No. 3.—A Deviation Line of Railway, commencing by a junction with the Sirhowy Tramroad, at or near the Twelve-and-Three-quarter Mile-post, on the said Sirhowy Tramroad, at Gellygroes, in the said parish of Mynyddyslwyn, and terminating by a junction with the Sirhowy Tramroad, at or near the Thirteen-and-a-quarter Mile-post, on the said Sirhowy Tramroad, in the said parish of Mynyddyslwyn.

No. 4.—A Junction Railway, commencing from and out of the Sirhowy Tramroad, at or near the Twelve-and-Three-quarter Mile-post, on the said Sirhowy Tramroad, in the said parish of Mynyddyslwyn, and terminating by a junction with the Newport, Abergavenny, and Hereford Railway, near the eastern end of the Tunnel on that Railway, nearest to the Tredegar Junction Station, and in the said parish of Mynyddyslwyn.

No. 5.—A Deviation Railway, commencing by a junction with the said Sirhowy Tramroad, at or near the Thirteen-and-a-Half Mile-post, on the said Sirhowy Tramroad, in the said parish of Mynyddyslwyn, and terminating by a junction with the said Sirhowy Tramroad, at or near the Fourteen Mile-post, on the said Tramroad, in the parish of Bedwellty, in the same county.

No. 6 —A Deviation Railway commencing by a jun with the said Sirhowy Tramroad, at or near the said F teen and Three-quarter Mile-post on the said tram and terminating by a junction with the said Sirhowy T road at or near the Sixteen Mile-post on the said Sirh Tramroad, in the same parish of Bedwellty.

No. 7.—A Deviation Railway, commencing by a jun with the said Sirhowy Tramroad at or near the Six and a quarter Mile-post on the said tramroad, and te nating by a junction with the said tramroad at or nea Sixteen and Three-quarter Mile-post on the said tram in the same parish of Bedwellty.

No. 8.—A Deviation Railway, commencing by a j tion with the said tramroad at or near the Seventeen post on the said tramroad, in the same parish of Bedwe and terminating by a junction with the said tramro or near the Eighteen and a quarter Mile-post on the tramroad, in the same parish of Bedwellty.

No. 9 —A Deviation Railway, commencing by a j tion with the said tramroad at or near the Eighteen a quarter Mile-post on the said tramroad, in the same pa of Bedwellty, and terminating by a junction with the tramroad at or near the Nineteen and a Half Mile-po the said tramroad, in the same parish of Bedwellty.

No 10.—A Deviation Railway, commencing by a j tion with the said tramroad, at or near the Nineteen-a-Half Mile-post on the said tramroad, and terminatin a junction with the said tramroad, at or near the Twe and-a-Half Mile-post on the said tramroad, all in the s parish of Bedwellty.

No. 11.—A Deviation Railway, commencing by a j tion with the said Sirhowy Tramroad at or near the Tw and a half Mile-post on the said tramroad, in the parish of Bedwellty, and terminating at or near the sent northern terminus of the said Sirhowy Tramro

No. 12.—The widening of the Sirhowy Tramroad, mencing from a point at or near the Fourteen Mile-po the said tramroad, in the said parish of Bedwellty, terminating at a point at or near the Fourteen and T quarter Mile-post on the said tramroad, in the same p of Bedwellty, and the diversion or alteration of ce roads between such last-mentioned points. To carr said intended deviation railways, or some of them, p along or over the lines of the existing roads of the Com Which said intended railways and works will be ma pass from, in, through, or into the parishes and p following, or some of them, that is to say, Machen, Ma Upper, Machen Lower, Mynyddyslwyn, and Bedwe all in the county of Monmouth.

An extract from the Monmouthshire Canal Act of 26th June, 1802 (42 George III, Cap 115) for the Sirhowy Tramroad.

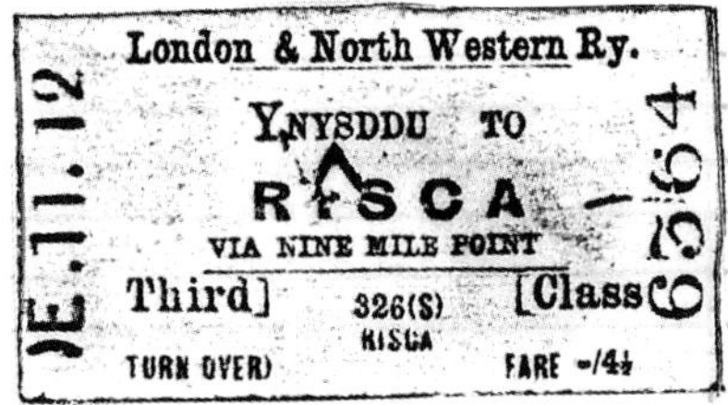

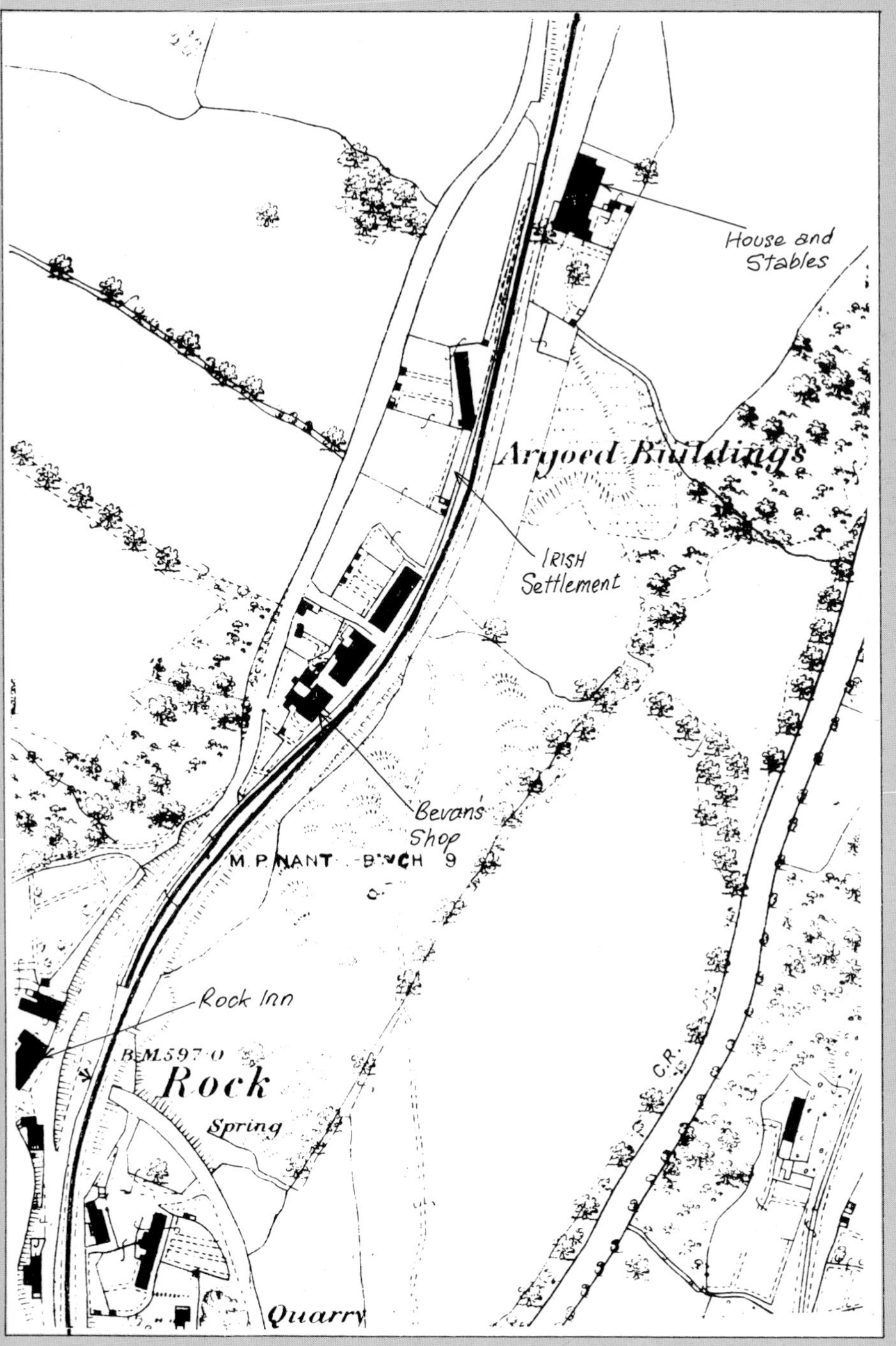

Argoed Buildings at Rock.
Reproduced from the Second Edition Ordnance Survey map c.1900

Above: Nos 11 and 12, Argoed buildings, Rock. No. 11 was Mrs Harriet Bevan's shop; the daughter of Thomas Ellis; the engineer for the Sirhowy Tramroad.
Left: The house and stables at Rock. Built by the tramroad and used for the changing of horses.
Below: Part of 'Argoed Buildings' at the Rock built for the employees of the Sirhowy Tramroad, now demolished.

All Courtesy, Mrs Olwen Hemming

The founders of the Tredegar Ironworks were seeking powers to provide easier transport, and a lease dated 20th March, 1800, from Sir Charles Morgan to the founders of the Tredegar Ironworks (Samuel Homfray, Richard Fothergill, and Matthew Monkhouse) gave full powers to Samuel Homfray and his co-partners 'to dig and trench in and upon the said lands for the purpose of getting Iron Ore and coal; including power to erect Engines, Furnaces, Forges etc. and to make tramways on any part of the said lands and over the same, down the Sirhowy Valley to join the Monmouthshire Canal'. In fact, a tramroad was constructed all the way to Pill on the banks of the River Usk at Newport.

The Monmouthshire Canal was already in use from Newport (Uskside) to Crumlin, in the Western Valley, so these proposals, quite understandably, were not acceptable to them. The Ironworks proprietors were approached again by the canal company, saying in effect, that if Homfray and his partners abandoned their scheme, the canal company would undertake, at its expense, to construct a tramroad from the Tredegar Works to a point on the canal near Risca church, on or before 25th December, 1801. The agreement was dated 18th December, 1800 between the canal company and Samuel Homfray and his partners. What was eventually sanctioned by Parliament in the Canal Act of 26th June, 1802 was vastly different from the original lease, in that it gave Homfray, Fothergill, Monkhouse, Thompson and Foreman, as Directors of the Sirhowy Tramroad Co., power to make at their own expense the 16 miles of tramroad from the Sirhowy Works to Nine Mile Point. The canal company built the remainder to the River Usk at Newport, except for the 'Park Mile' which was the responsibility of Sir Charles Morgan.

A stone bridge crossed the valley at Risca on the Monmouthshire Canal Co's section. A carriageway ran alongside the tramway from Penllwyn Mawr to Tredegar, with no fence between them. The wagons or trams averaged about 17 cwt. tare each, had no springs or buffers, and were connected by stiff drawbars. Horses used on the tramroad were the finest obtainable – a new horse on the scene brought excitement and speculation to the boys of Argoed and Blackwood! Stabling for the horses was made at Tredegar, the Rock (situated between Argoed and Blackwood), Nine Mile Point and Danygraig, Risca. The Nine Mile Point building later became the station master's house. It was situated just south of the up platform, and to give adequate clearance had 18 inches taken off the front of it when the line was doubled. After veterinary treatment, many horses found their way to Lower Farm, between Tredegar and Hollybush, where they spent their convalescence before returning to Tredegar and work again.

Sprags kept the trams under control on their downward journey – this was most essential as runaway trams could kill the horses instantly. The rule of the road was simple; no wagon must have less than four wheels, and their speed must not exceed 4 mph. Empty wagons had to give way to loaded wagons. Due to tramplate breakages, an 1806 regulation restricted the total weight of the laden wagon to 56 cwt.

From roughly 1810 onwards the tramroad could be used by private carriers, on payment of a toll as on the turnpike roads. A passenger service was

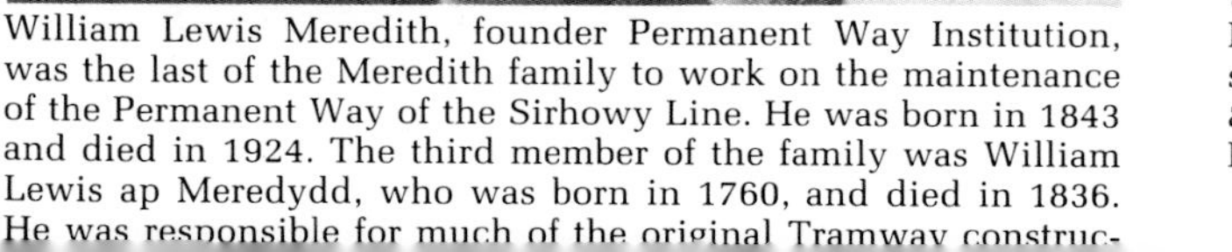

William Lewis Meredith, founder Permanent Way Institution, was the last of the Meredith family to work on the maintenance of the Permanent Way of the Sirhowy Line. He was born in 1843 and died in 1924. The third member of the family was William Lewis ap Meredydd, who was born in 1760, and died in 1836. He was responsible for much of the original Tramway construc-

Mrs Harriet Bevan, wife of Walter Bevan. Mr Bevan was a noted surveyor and a partner in the Rhoswen Colliery Co. of Bevan & Pryce in the 1870's. Mrs Bevan (daughter of Thomas Ellis, Engineer, Tredegar) kept the Rhoswen Shop at the Rock.

Courtesy of Mrs Olwen Hemming

introduced in 1822 by John Kingston of Newport. This horse-drawn vehicle was known locally as the Caravan. Slater's 1850 Directory mentions a service from Newport to Tredegar by Henry Morgan (per Tramroad). There was also the 'Waterloo Coach' run by George Stokes and John Williams on Wednesdays and Saturdays from the Rose & Thistle. Mails to Newport went by Royal Mail from Tredegar Arms every morning at 8.30 am. The 'Directory' also mentions Thomas Ellis, Sen. Civil Engineer, Church Street, Tredegar. Thomas Ellis was responsible for the building of the many steam locomotives during the tramroad period from 1830 to 1860, and afterwards worked as a free-lance engineer.

In 1800 Benjamin Outram advised the company with regard to the permanent way and recommended the use of flanged iron tramplates on stone blocks and laid with their inner faces 4 ft 2 in. apart.

A description of the Tramroad by T.G. Cumming in 1824 reads as follows:

> In the county of Monmouth, the Sirhoway rail-way forms one of the first, in point of magnitude, which has hitherto been constructed. It extends from Pilgwelly, near Newport, to the Sirhoway and Tredegar iron works, a distance of 24 miles, whence it is continued five miles further to the Trevil lime works, in Breckonshire, along with a branch to the west to the Rumney and Union iron works. This rail-way was constructed at the suggestion of Mr Outram, engineer. On being consulted by the Monmouthshire canal company, as to the best means of supplying that canal with water, of which they experienced so great a scarcity, particularly in the Crumlyn line, that the trade was suffering very severely from the circumstance, this gentleman recommended a few reservoirs to be made, but more particularly a tram road to run parallel with the Crumlin line, for eight or nine miles from the town of Newport. In order to ease or take away part of the trade from the canal, this line was to pass through Tredegar Park, the property of Sir Charles Morgan, Bart, and it was finally arranged between Sir Charles, and the Monmouthshire canal company, and the Tredegar iron works company, that he should make one mile, which was within his park, the Monmouthshire canal company to make eight miles and the Tredegar iron company to make the remaining 15 miles, each to take tonnage on their respective parts of the road.
>
> This rail-way was completed about twenty years ago, also a turnpike road by the side of it for about 17 miles, the total expense amounting to about £74,000, or about £3,000 per mile. About £40,000 of this sum was expended by the canal company in consequence of building a bridge, and some very deep and expensive cutting, whilst the Tredegar iron company completed nearly double the distance at the cost of £30,000. Sir Charles Morgan expended £4,000 upon one mile, but he had some deep cutting, and a double road to make. Notwithstanding the expense, this road pays the proprietors 30 per cent, having a considerable trade upon it in coal and iron, which pay the same tonnage as the canal. For the first nine miles out of Newport, being the parts made by Sir Charles Morgan and the canal company, it is a double road; one for the loaded waggons to come down, and the other one for the empty ones to return; and on the Tredegar iron company's part of 15 miles, it is a single road, with frequent turn outs for the teams to pass. The whole line of the road for 24 miles is an inclined plane, averaging about the eighth of an inch in the yard, or something more; but that part made by the Tredegar iron company is of somewhat greater declivity than the rest. The coal and iron are conveyed upon it in waggons, each carrying about forty-five to fifty hundred weight, exclusive of the waggon; and a team of four or five horses will draw about fifteen of these waggons down and take the same number of empty ones back, with ease. The waggons are

variously constructed according to the fancy of the parties some are made of wood, and others wholly of iron; the latter are, however, now more generally approved of. The weight of them is as various as their construction. That part of the road made by the Monmouthshire canal company crosses a valley at Risca, seven miles from Newport, by a bridge of near forty arches, and from forty to fifty feet high. This is a noble monument of the spirit and industry of Britons.

The width of the road is 4 ft 2 in. composed of cast-iron plates, in 3 ft lengths, having a flaunche on the plate, and not on the wheel, forming nearly the angle of a square, the flaunche inclining a little inwards. The sleepers are stout blocks of stone, firmly bedded in the ground, with the extremities of each adjoining rail resting upon them, and made fast thereto by a pin passing through the rail, and into a hole bored in the block four or five inches deep, and there secured with lead.

The Meredith family, of Argoed maintained the Sirhowy Tramroad from its inception in 1800. William Lewis ap Meredydd was born in 1760, William Meredith born in 1809 and William Lewis Meredith was born in 1843. They were a very old family and the paternal ancestors were descended from Llewelyn, third son of Gwilym ap Philip of Rhiwbina, by Cardiff, who settled at Gwrhay, in the Parish of Mynyddislwyn, Monmouthshire, *c.*1425. William Lewis Meredith later founded the Permanent Way Institution.

In a private letter, dated 28th December, 1905, written to the GWR's District Goods Manager at Cardiff, William Lewis Meredith stated:

The main Sirhowy Tram-road from the Canal at Newport, i.e. from Cwyndau, behind the Castle of Newport, the old Dock Street Station, by the Gaer, through Tredegar Park to the Nine Mile Point and on to Tredegar and Sirhowy Iron Works, then called Sirhowy Furnaces, was constructed mostly by my grandfather, William Lewis Meredith, between the years 1800 and 1811. This tramway was opened and brought into use on or about the 11th of August 1811;* parts of it were in use by the Tredegar and Sirhowy Ironworks Companies before this date, the tram-road from Sirhowy Furnaces to Trevil and Bryn Oer Mines was made about the years 1795 to 1800.

My Grandfather, Father and myself were employed continuously from about the year 1795 to the year 1875 in the making, maintaining and reconstructions of the Sirhowy Tram-roads from the commencement or first beginning of the tramways to the Limestone Quarries at Trevil in Brecknockshire. In the year 1873 the Tredegar Iron and Coal Company purchased the Ironworks and mineral property as well as the Sirhowy Railway and its Tram-road Branches from the old Company of proprietors. The Sirhowy Railway was shortly afterwards disposed of to the London and North Western Railway Company.

I acquired my early training on the Sirhowy Tram-roads and at the Tredegar Iron Works and assisted in the work of maintaining the tram-roads of the whole system as also of their several renewals and reconstructions until the Railway was opened as a public passenger line (in June of 1865), a period extending from 1854 to 1866.

I am well acquainted with the early history, customs and trade developments of the works and manufactures and their owners, carried on throughout the Sirhowy Valley and its neighbourhood. The traffic over this Tramway in the earliest days was conveyed by Horse-power. The Tredegar Iron Company, the Sirhowy and

*'There is not necessarily a discrepancy between this and the other statements [e.g. Cumming, 1824], as Meredith specified [elsewhere] *public* use, and it is probable that earlier use was for the exclusive benefit of the Tredegar & Sirhowy Works' (Charles E. Lee, *Railway Magazine* Sept. 1939).

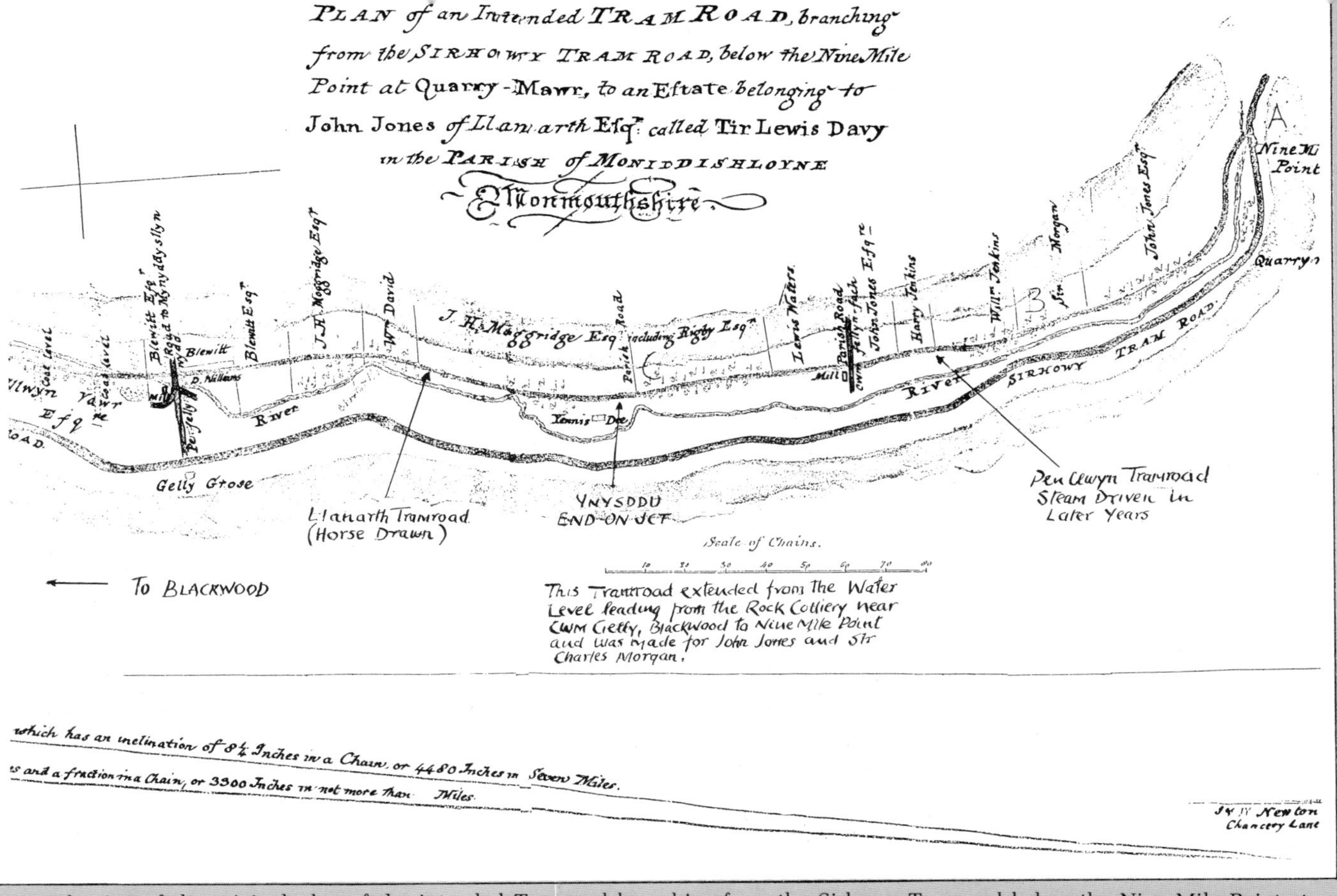

A reproduction of the original plan of the intended Tramroad branching from the Sirhowy Tramroad below the Nine Mile Point at Quarry mawr.
Author's Collection

> Ebbw Vale Iron and Coal Companies, began using steam power over this tram-road about the year 1830, the Locomotive engines being of similar type to Stephenson's earliest engines – the 'Rocket' type. In addition to these the Ebbw Vale Company used engines from the Sirhowy Works of different mechanical design, being propelled by means of a cross-beam after the manner of a pumping Stationary engine. For some years the traffic over the Tram-road was simultaneously conducted with Locomotive Steam Power and Horse-power, and to prevent collisions, the chimneys of the Locomotive Engines were kept white-lime-washed so as to be easily seen from a distance by trains and Horse-teams and Passengers trams coming along the tram-road in the opposite directions. This custom of working the tram-roads between Newport and Sirhowy continued until the Monmouthshire Canal Company converted their tram-road system in the Western Valleys into a public railway system, which previously had been used by the various Ironworks Companies, Colliery Companies and Proprietors, farmers, land-owners, and others to convey goods and passengers by horse-power. The Sirhowy Tram-road Company and the Canal Company and other owners of tram-roads charging the tolls for minerals, merchandise and passengers, they were authorised to charge under the Act of Parliament referred to [1802].

A booklet written by William Lewis Meredith and printed by Derry & Sons Ltd, Nottingham, in 1907, *The Tramroads of the Sirhowy Valley (In Gwent-Uchcoed), Newport to Sirhowy etc., Monmouthshire, 1795 to 1855* provides further interesting reading. Part of it is quoted below:

> The Sirhowy Valley commences at the junction of the Sirhowy River with the Ebbw River near Risca, about 6½ miles to the north of the Port Town of Newport. The Gwentlan natives (15th–18th century) called the River and spelled it CORRWY or CORWY. Later it became SORWY or SIRHOWEY, and finally its modern SIRHOWY. The small village of Argoed is still known as Cwm Corrwg. The village of Argoed is of modern date and does not appear to have existed when Coxe wrote his History.

Meredith refers to the following tramroads in the Sirhowy Valley:

> 1 The Monmouthshire Canal Company Tramroad from Newport.
> 2 The Sirhowy Main Tramroad from Nine Mile Point to the Sorrwy Furnaces, and the Cwm Gelli branches near Blackwood.
> 3 The Sirhowy branch from Nine Mile Point to Ynysddu.
> 4 The Penllwyn Branch from the Sirhowy Tramroad to a junction about 4½ miles from Nine Mile Point to the village of Bryn, and thence to the Gelli-Haf Coal Level.
> 5 The Llanarth Tramway from the junction with the Sirhowy Tramroad at Ynysddu to the Rock Coal Level at Charles-Town, Blackwood.
>
> The Sirhowy Tramroad No. 2 and its branch roads Nos. 3 and 4 were made under the authority of an Act of Parliament obtained by the Monmouthshire Canal Company in the years 1792, 1797 and 1802, to make a canal from near a place called Cryndau Farm, near Newport to or near Crumlin Bridge (not the viaduct).
>
> The Sirhowy Tramroad Company ceased to run their trains to Newport about the time the Canal Company converted their Western Valley Tramway into a public railway, which was opened as a passenger railway in the year 1851.
>
> The Sirhowy Tramroad Company about the same time commenced running passenger trains on their tramroad, and continued for a short while – a few days or about a week, consisting of locomotive engine and three passenger coaches, to Tredegar, the wheels of the engine and train being adapted to travel on the edge-rail and tramplate simultaneously. These passenger trains were discontinued

An original engraving of the 'Fatal Explosion' at Bedwellty Pits Colliery, near Tredegar, Monmouthshire.

Author's Collection

within a week or two, but whether by order of the Board of Trade or through breakages of the cast iron tram-plates, which still formed portions of the tram-road, I cannot now state, probably the former, as the Canal Company's Acts, under which the tramroads were authorised, contained no mention of passenger tolls, although for years previously private owners of horse trams carried passengers from the villages in the Sirhowy Valley.

To return to earlier days; the increase in traffic brought problems for the Tredegar Iron Company, and their attention had been drawn to the 'steam travelling engine' in the north. Samuel Homfray ceased his iron making activities in 1818 to enter the House of Commons as a member for Stafford, but his son – also Samuel Homfray, then 23 years old was found to be quite capable of looking after the company's affairs. His son was also interested in steam power since he had seen the famous Richard Trevithick at Penydarren, Merthyr in 1804, with his 'High Pressure' engine. He now gave the Stephensons details of the Sirhowy Tramroad, and its possible traffic, and after discussion on both sides, it was decided to send Thomas Ellis, the engineer appointed by the company in 1828 to Killingworth, to see the engines produced there. With him went Theophilus Jones, a mining agent. The result of this visit was an order from Homfray for a locomotive (named *Britannia*) to run on the Sirhowy Tramroad.

The engine started working in the vicinity of Tredegar works in October 1829 and made its first journey to Newport just before Christmas of that year, taking Homfray and many of his friends to Sir Charles Morgan's cattle show at Court-y-bella Farm, Newport. The engine, about 9 tons in weight, 'possessed the somewhat stark appearance of being simply a round boiler resting on three pairs of wheels with a small smoke stack curving up from the front'. Although the start from Tredegar was made at day-break, it was dark by the time they had reached Bassaleg, about a mile and a half from Newport. The engine seemed too heavy for the tram-plates, causing some breakages, and the fixed wheelbase of the engine knocked the tramroad about on sharp curves and junctions. Finally, going through Tredegar Park, the chimney collided with the overhanging branches of a tree and was broken. Later, with her teething troubles over, *Britannia* became a good worker, making daily journeys of 28 miles with tram loads of 50 and 60 tons and reducing the cost of horse traction by 35 per cent.

About this time, two other locomotives made their appearance on the tramway; they were *Speedwell* and *Hercules*, built by the Neath Abbey Ironworks for the colliery proprietor and town clerk of Newport, Thomas Prothero. There were still difficulties however, in operating and consequent damage to tramplates, with the result that the Monmouthshire Canal Company issued the following statement in 1830:

> With a view to save the breakage of tramplates and to prevent the consequent interruption of the freighters generally, resolved that no locomotive steam engine be allowed to travel on this company's tramroads that is not suspended on proper springs.

The locomotives designed and built by Thomas Ellis for the Tredegar Iron Company between 1832 and 1853 were named *St David*, *Tredegar*, *Jane*,

ANNO VICESIMO TERTIO

VICTORIÆ REGINÆ.

****

Cap. lxxi.

An Act for changing the Name of the *Sirhowy* Tramroad Company to the Name "The *Sirhowy* Railway Company," and for authorizing the Company to make new Works, and to maintain and work the *Sirhowy* Line as a Railway, and to raise further Funds, and for regulating their Capital and Borrowing Powers; and for other Purposes. [25th *May* 1860.]

WHEREAS an Act (in this Act called "the Act of 1792") was passed in the Thirty-second Year of *George* the Third, Chapter 102, (Local,) intituled *An Act for making and maintaining a navigable Cut or Canal from, or from some Place near,* Pontnewynydd *into the River* Usk *at or near the Town of* Newport, *and a collateral Cut or Canal from the same at or near a Place called* Cryndau Farm, *to or near to* Crumlin Bridge, *all in the County of* Monmouth, *and for making and maintaining Railways or Stoneroads from such Cuts or Canals to several Ironworks and Mines in the Counties of* Monmouth *and* Brecknock, whereby a Company, therein called "the Company of Proprietors of the *Monmouthshire* Canal Navigation," but since and now

32 G. 3. c. cii.

[*Local.*] 10 *N* called

The first page of the Act which permitted the Tramroad to become a standard gauge railway.

Lord Rodney, *Lady Sale*, *Prince Albert*, *Fanny*, *Charlotte* (named after Homfray's wife) and *Bedwellty*. There is also a record of another engine named *Laura*, built in 1848. (It should be noted that the Sirhowy Tramroad Company did not provide locomotives of its own.) These engines were about 13 tons each, with 4-wheel tenders of 5½ tons each. It is recorded that on 18th April, 1848 the *St David*, which had recently been rebuilt, hauled a train of 179 tons 19 cwt; a vast improvement on the horse-drawn traction of the 1820s. The *Bedwellty* was built in 1853, and was in traffic locally until 1882, but was not scrapped until some years later. The smokebox end of the engines was whitewashed each week so that they could easily be sighted in traffic. It seems Ellis trained several prominent apprentices at Tredegar including the man who became the chief locomotive superintendent of the GWR, and later its Chairman, Sir Daniel Gooch.

The transitional period, when the tramway was converted from a plateway to a railway for the use of the flanged wheel, gave endless difficulties. Some were still using the flangeless wheel (various connections with the main tramway) while at other points the ordinary standard gauge flanged wheels were in use. These difficulties were experienced at Tredegar Junction, Nine Mile Point and several other places. To ease matters during this period, a combined wrought iron plate and Great Western 'Bridge' pattern rail of heavy section, was brought into use. This combined plate and rail had a wide inner tread for unflanged wheels at 4 ft 2 in. gauge and a raised outer portion for ordinary standard gauge flanged wheels. The rail proved effective in the interim period until the proper conversion under the Act of 25th May, 1860 which changed the name of the undertaking from the Sirhowy Tramroad Company to the Sirhowy Railway Company, and authorised the conversion of the line into a standard gauge railway. The Act also gave the company powers to build an extension from Sirhowy to Nantybwch to join the Merthyr, Tredegar & Abergavenny Railway with a junction facing Merthyr, but this was amended later under an Act of 5th June, 1865 for a junction facing Abergavenny. The Directors for the company were Samuel Homfray, Watkin Homfray, Rowland Fothergill, and William Forman.

Reverting back for a moment to the early part of the 19th century, one of the first tramroad turnouts at the lower end of the valley was near the Risca long bridge going to the Danygraig Copper Works. A Birmingham company opened a smelting plant for non-ferrous metals in 1807, the only plant of its kind in Monmouthshire, built on land leased from the Morgan family for 99 years and capable of smelting 10,000 tons of copper ore per annum. The Copper Works was working as a chemical plant in 1842 under David Morris. By 1860 the latter had additional plants at Ynysddu (Duffryn) and Abercarn, where there were sidings. Morris died in 1880, when the plants were taken over by Capt. W.M. Morgan. In 1892 the buildings at Danygraig were converted for the manufacture of bricks. The Risca long bridge of 32 arches was by-passed by a deviation on a long embankment authorised by the Monmouthshire Railway & Canal Company's Act of 1853, and was out of use by 1855 when the line was modernised to Nine Mile Point.

There were several boiler explosions in the early tramroad days. In March

1830 a boiler burst killing a boy working on the side of the tramroad at Tredegar and in July of the same year, Thomas Jones, described as a 'tram engine fireman', was killed by an explosion. Looking through back numbers of *The Monmouthshire Merlin* it seems there were many collisions after the introduction of steam power, and Beer Houses alongside the tramroad were blamed for many of the accidents. This comes from the 29th March, 1843 edition:

> On Saturday evening last at 5.30 pm as the Vulcan Steam Engine and trams (the property of the Tredegar Iron Company) was returning from Newport when nearly opposite the George Inn, Blackwood, the boiler bursting and occasioned the lives of Mr W. Davies, Farmer, formerly of Buttery Hatch, and Mr Phillip Jones, of Blackwood, who was standing near the corner and opposite where the engine stood. Mr Davies was upwards of 80 years old. All the glass was smashed in the George Inn. A man named James Hale who was standing on the footplate escaped injury as part of the boiler went over his head!
>
> Samuel Homfray Esq of Tredegar said all expenses would be met. Value of Engine £500.
>
> Inquest held at Royal Oak, Blackwood by W. Brewer Esq.

Mary Lloyd of the Argoed Arms Public House was killed on Monday, 23rd August, 1858 when a tram she was riding on overturned on the common above Argoed. She had been to Tredegar this day and was returning to Argoed. At the Inquest, held at the Rock Inn, it was stated that the tyre of the tender wheel had come off and the train was thrown down the embankment. The last tram fell upon Abraham Richards and Mary Lloyd. She was later found dead under the tram. Robert Jones, smith to the Tredegar Company, reported that he had put on the tyre within a fortnight, and that it was properly put on. William Meredith proved that the road was in good condition and that he had examined it a quarter of an hour before the accident had occurred.

One interesting matter is the inventive genious behind the construction of points – known then as 'partings' in South Wales. In the early days difficulty was experienced in getting a tram from one road to another in local collieries and levels, and on the Tramroad. The alleged experiences of Mr Fothergill and Mr Homfray on these matters brings, to say the least, confusion, if nothing else! One story comes from Powell's *History of Tredegar*, and relates a curious incident which occurred to 'Old Mr Fothergill' one Sunday morning at Waunypond church. Mr Fothergill was very punctual and attentive at Waunypond church, but at the time of constructing tramroads at Sirhowy works the old gentleman's inventive faculties had been strained and taxed to extremes. Partings and crossings were not invented, which was an insurmountable difficulty when roads were required to be constructed in various directions. The old gentleman pondered and planned, crossings and partings were playing on his mind in the works, in the house, and in the church. But on the said Sunday morning, the floor of the church was adorned with a thick coat of strewn sawdust. While the Reverend 'Price Bach' was proceeding with the morning service, Mr Fothergill was seen drawing a plan with the point of his staff in the sawdust, and at last ejaculated, 'That is it . . .'

[39 & 40 VICT.] *The London and North-western* [Ch. cxxxiii.]
Railway (Sirhowy Railway Vesting) Act, 1876.

CHAPTER cxxxiii.

An Act for vesting in the London and North-western Railway Company the Undertaking of the Sirhowy Railway Company. [13th July 1876.]

A.D. 1876.

WHEREAS by the Act (local and personal) 42 Geo. 3. c. 115. a Company was incorporated under the name or title of the Sirhowy Tramroad Company, and by the Act (local and personal) 23 & 24 Vict. c. 71. the name of that Company was changed to the Sirhowy Railway Company (in this Act called the Sirhowy Company), and under and by virtue of those Acts and the Act (local and personal) 28 & 29 Vict. c. 342. they have constructed and completed the railways and works by those Acts or some of them authorised:

42 Geo. 3. c. cxv.

23 & 24 Vict. c. lxxi.

28 & 29 Vict. c. cccxlii.

And whereas the railway of the Sirhowy Company forms a junction near Tredegar with the Merthyr, Tredegar, and Abergavenny Railway of the London and North-western Railway Company (in this Act called the Company), and there is a considerable interchange of traffic between the railways of the two Companies:

And whereas the Company and the Sirhowy Company have agreed for the vesting in the former Company of the undertaking of the latter Company, upon the terms and conditions contained in the agreement set forth in the schedule to this Act, and it would be of advantage to the two Companies and of great public and local convenience if the undertaking of the Sirhowy Company were transferred to and vested in the Company accordingly:

And whereas the capital of the Sirhowy Company consists of one thousand and fifty ordinary shares of one hundred pounds each, fully paid up, and of ninety thousand pounds of preference stock, eighteen thousand pounds of which is yet unissued, and they have borrowed on mortgage, and there is now due, the sum of fifty-six thousand six hundred and thirty-three pounds:

And whereas the objects of this Act cannot be attained without the authority of Parliament:

[*Local.–133.*]

The Sirhowy Railway was taken over by the LNWR in 1876.

Whereupon the officiating clergyman paused; the old gentleman lifted up his head, and with a smile said, 'Go on Mr Price, it is all right now,' and the plan of the crossing had been completed.

Another account of how points and crossings were invented comes from the book *Reflections on a Railway Career* by the late J.M. Dunn, and was originally told by a former Vicar of Usk in Monmouthshire – Canon D. Ivor Jones.

> At the time of the construction of the Sirhowy Tramroad, the problem of transferring vehicles from one set of metals to another while in motion had not been solved and was engaging the whole-hearted attention of Mr Homfray. This gentleman was a regular worshipper at St Georges Church, Tredegar, which, in those days, had the floor covered in sand. During the sermon one Sunday Mr Homfray, I am sorry to relate, had allowed his attention to wander from the things of the spirit, and to return to those of Iron and Steel, and he was busy drawing a set of railway lines on the sanded floor with his walking stick. Suddenly, to everyones' horror – his own included, no doubt – he shouted at the top of his voice, 'Damn it, I've got it'. He had discovered how to make a pair of points.

Was it sand or sawdust? My choice, if any, would be sawdust and old Mr Fothergill. St George's at Tredegar was built in 1836 and I believe the construction of points and crossings had been settled long before then.

A display made by the Tredegar Iron & Coal Co Ltd showing their equipment available, obviously constructed and assembled in the works before being displayed at a show. *Author's Collection*

TREDEGAR. LNWR.

A commercial postcard view of 1920 showing station, engine shed and yards of Tredegar station, LNWR. *Lens of Sutton*

A view of the station, engine shed at Tredegar station in the 1920s. *Lens of Sutton*

Chapter Two

The Town of Tredegar

Although the railway's name is taken from what was originally the small village of Sirhowy and the Valley's river, the story hinges almost entirely on the town of Tredegar.

There was no housing of any consequence prior to the building of the first furnaces in the area. The Sirhowy Iron Works was founded in 1778 by four businessmen who leased land from Charles Henry Burgh, with a yearly rental of £134 9s. A few years later the Works was taken over by Richard Fothergill and Matthew Monkhouse, and in 1800 Samuel Homfray joined them to establish the Tredegar Iron Works.

An agreement dated 26th June, 1802 split the Tramroad construction to Newport into three parts: The Tredegar Iron Works (Samuel Homfray & Partners) to make the Tramroad from Tredegar to Nine Mile Point; the Monmouthshire Canal Company responsible from Nine Mile Point to the River Usk at Newport, except the 'Park Mile', which was the responsibility of Sir Charles Morgan.

The Sirhowy Tramroad was the first major work in the valley, and came at a time when local landowners were invaded by prospectors who bought or leased ground with mineral rights, and coal levels began to appear rapidly in the valley. The first Pit in the area was Dukes Pit, in 1806, when the coal was raised by Water Balance; to be followed by many others in quick succession. The Industrial Revolution brought endless opportunities to Tredegar. With all the necessary raw materials available, the Iron and Steel industry forged ahead rapidly. Coal was mined in large quantities, and brick making was also carried on at a large rate. Every conceivable form of equipment was made for use in the furnaces and underground for the collieries. (See *page 23* for a selection of the variety of items available.) Steel sleepers and bullhead section rail was also manufacturered. Tredegar was indeed a very busy and thriving town.

In the autumn of 1873 James Colquhoun was appointed Manager of the Iron Works, and vast improvements were made, including the construction of the company's own railway system. The Tredegar Iron & Coal Company began to run their own workman's trains to the Whitworth, Ty Trist and Bedwellty Pits Collieries over their own metals and by their own locomotives.

While all this was going on there were complaints from the public of the appalling conditions of the industrial towns in South Wales; the various guides gave the distinct impression of dirt and grime everywhere and of the primitive housing and health hazards involved and Tredegar was no exception! This report from a contemporary Newspaper was typical of many at the time:

> Complaints are received daily about haphazard driving through the streets of Tredegar – little children run in dozens after the trams and on one occasion the Trevil engine brought about 60 trams and came to a halt across the main road near Colliers Row. The Rev'd Edmund Leigh, Rector of Bedwellty had a narrow escape as he tried to cross. Break-downs and runaways are common.

Other accounts may be found in *Murray's Guide* of 1872:

> With the exception of Nantyglo, Tredegar certainly bears the palm of being the dirtiest and most unpleasant town in all the iron districts of South Wales. The

A view of Tredegar signal box, level crossing and station in 1904. *Courtesy the late Oliva Ashton*

A busy yard scene with 'posing' station staff in 1920 at Tredegar station; LNWR Coal Tank and close-coupled set await next duty. *Courtesy Mrs Jean Burr*

A further fine 1920s view of Tredegar Crossing signal box (known as 'No. 1 Signal Box') and station with two LNWR Coal Tanks standing on the crossing. This was the only signal box in the area with an eight hour shift; the rest were working a ten-hour shift system.

Courtesy Mrs Jean Burr

> streets are intersected by tramroads, along which many little skeleton engines, dangerous alike to life and traffic, are perpetually bringing coal to the furnaces. In the Market-Place is a tall ugly clock-tower, the gift of a former Manager.

and in the Official Guide to the LNWR, 1885:

> Advancing through mining surroundings we come to Beaufort, the changing station for Ebbw Vale, and its great iron industry. Then by rough hill summits, bare fields, and heaps of rubbish, giving the whole district an air of indescribable dreariness, we pass Trevil and Nantybwch, the junction for the Sirhowy branch, which serves Sirhowy, where are large collieries and works for the manufacture of pig-iron; Tredegar, a modern and populous iron town, owing its rise and progress to the Tredegar Iron & Coal Company Ltd, who here employ some four thousand hands; and on by Bedwellty Pits, Holly Bush, Argoed and Blackwood, to Tredegar Junction, thence Ynysddu, Nine Mile Point, Risca and Bassaleg to Newport, (High Street).

The 'North Western' did not have a very happy relationship with the local authority, and one subject which was never far away was the everlasting problem of the railway level crossing and the continuous hold-ups by road traffic at the gates. Public meetings were held over many years – the railway company preferred a subway; the local authority wanted a roadbridge over all lines; those of the railway company and of the Tredegar Iron & Coal Co, which ran parallel. All the public got in the end was a footbridge!

There were rumours in the 1920s that the locomotive sheds were to be transferred to a new site at Pontllanfraith, and later, of a new station for Blackwood, near the town centre; also a new waiting room and overbridge at Markham Village. Most of these projects were soon forgotten. Another bombshell for Tredegar was the removal of Messrs Whitehead Iron & Steel Works from Tredegar to a site at Newport; Mr Whitehead stressed that the Newport site was far more convenient as the LNWR had the monopoly at Tredegar. He said traffic could reach London in a day; whereas it took three or four times as long from Tredegar!

Tredegar's famous landmark, The Clock Tower in the 'Circle'. The clock itself was designed by J.B. Joyce, clock makers, of Whitchurch, Salop, a firm who made clocks for many railway companies including the LNWR, and clocks in the Sirhowy Valley. Overall design was by James Watson, whereas all the ironwork was cast in the Foundry of Charles Jordan, of Newport, and was erected in 1859. *Author's Collection*

The area around Tredegar.

Reduced and reproduced from the 1904, 6″ Ordnance Survey Map

Tredegar Station Staff 1909. *Courtesy the late Olive Ashton*

Pre-grouping photograph of the original station at Tredegar (rebuilt 1932). The track in foreground leads to the Tredegar Iron & Coal Company's Ironworks (*left*) and to the Whitworth, Ty Trist, and Bedwellty Collieries to the right. *G. Davies*

LNWR 'Coal' Tank, No. 429 and a five coach close-coupled set at Tredegar station in 1909. The locomotive was built in 1886; Crewe No. 2925 (Duplicate list No. 3414), LMS No. 7764, and was withdrawn February 1936. *Courtesy the late Oliva Ashton*

Long colliers' train loading at Pochin Colliery platform. The train consists of mixed 4- and 6-wheeled stock. *Courtesy, Dr Gerwyn Thomas, National Museum of Wales*

Another view of colliers' train at Pochin Pits, showing the only woman worker (arrowed) amongst the colliers awaiting to board the train. *Gerald Davies*

Chapter Three

Conversion to a Railway

The new standard gauge railway line was re-routed from Sirhowy to Bedwellty Pits and avoided the high streets at Argoed and Blackwood, along which the Tramway had run, going to the backs of the houses and cutting off their long gardens. The Sirhowy Railway Company was given three years to complete the conversion. The Monmouthshire line from Nine Mile Point to Newport was completed as a railway in 1855, and it was over this section that the Sirhowy Railway Co. was granted running powers when the latter commenced its passenger service from Sirhowy to Newport (Dock Street) on 19th June, 1865.

Originally, a change of carriage was to have taken place at Nine Mile Point into trains of the Monmouthshire Railway & Canal Co., but because of the inconvenience caused, the 1860 Act was superceded by the Sirhowy Railway Act of 5th July, 1865, which stipulated that three trains each way were to be run daily (except Sundays) between Tredegar and Newport 'without break or change of carriage'.

These trains were made up of three 4-wheel coaches and a 2–4–0 tank engine, with a choice of 1st, 2nd, and 3rd class travel, and started at Sirhowy, calling at Tredegar, Blackwood, Tredegar Junction, Risca, and ran into Newport (Dock Street) station. There were two Sunday trains each way, and one each way between Tredegar and Sirhowy. Argoed station opened in 1866 and Nine Mile Point in 1867. The journey took an average 1 h. 20 min. It seems the Sunday service ceased when the LNWR took over in 1875–76.

The extension from Sirhowy to Nantybwch to join the Merthyr, Tredegar & Abergavenny Line opened to the public on 2nd November, 1868. William Jones and John Saunders worked together as driver and guard for many years – Saunders was transferred to the LNWR in 1876 and continued working into the 1890s.

The Sirhowy Railway locomotives taken over by the LNWR in 1876 were numbered from 1 to 9, as listed below:

Sirhowy No.	*LNW No.*	*Maker*	*Maker's No.*	*Date*
1	1847	Slaughter & Co.	–	1863
2	1865	Slaughter & Co.	–	1863
3	1870	Vulcan Foundry	434	1860
4	1854	Vulcan Foundry	625	1871
5	1991	Vulcan Foundry	504	1863
6	1992	Vulcan Foundry	424	1859
7	1990	Vulcan Foundry	425	1859
8	1859	Vulcan Foundry	340	1866
9	1891	Worcester Engine Co.	–	1868

Nos. 1 & 2 were used as passenger engines, and were painted green with polished brass domes. They were side tank engines with 4 ft 6 in. coupled wheels, and 3 ft diameter leading wheels, and of the 2–4–0 wheel arrangement. Cylinders were 14 in. × 18 in., and the tanks carried 500 gallons of water. No. 1 weighed 22 tons, and No. 2, 23 tons 10 cwt. Numbers 3 to 7 were extremely awkward-looking saddle tanks, having 6-coupled wheels of 4 ft diameter, all situated in front of the firebox. Outside cylinders were 16 in. × 24 in., and the tank carried 960 gallons of water, and bunker 28 cwt. of coal. No. 8 was also a 6-wheel coupled saddle tank, but differed in that one pair of coupled wheels were placed behind the firebox. The coupled wheels were 4 ft 6 in. diameter.

Most of these engines had link motion and boiler feed pumps worked by eccentrics from the middle axle. All were built without cabs, with only a weatherplate to protect the driver. No. 9 was a 6-wheel coupled side tank engine purchased in 1873 from the Metropolitan Railway. The engine had double frames, 4 ft 3 in. wheels and 20 in. × 24 in. cylinders. The total weight was 45 tons. The engine was acquired in 1877 by the Alexandra Docks & Railway, Newport, and on this line was numbered 9, then 26. It was rebuilt with a new boiler and smaller cylinders of 18 in. diameter in 1921 by Messrs Hawthorne, Leslie & Co., Newcastle-on-Tyne, who, at the same time converted it into a 0–6–2 engine. In the following year the GWR took over the Alexandra Docks line, and classified the engine as A14, and altered its number to 663.

According to a diary kept by Gwillim Jenkins, a mason employed under contract by the company from 1866 to 1874, the brick arches of the Sirhowy engines were subject to frequent collapse during use, and in one instance No. 6 was rebricked three times in a year. On this subject there was considerable correspondence between the company and the Vulcan Works at Warrington. Gwillim Jenkins also did most of the masonry at Tredegar and places below, including a platform at Argoed, Blackwood, Tredegar Junction, and Nine Mile Point. The diary also mentions the construction of a signal box and waiting room at Tredegar Junction, as well as masonry for a water tank at Argoed and the well for a locomotive turntable at Tredegar. A house and workshop (since removed) existed at the Rock, between Argoed and Blackwood, where Ruben Pritchard repaired Sirhowy Company wagons.

Traces of Sirhowy property could still be seen at Blackwood and Pontllanfraith and various other places in 1960. A Sirhowy Company cast-iron plate was visible on a gate near the Rock in 1938.

The Sirhowy Railway Company began negotiations in 1874 with the Monmouthshire Company, and later with the Great Western, for the sale of the company. The GWR were anxious to acquire the Sirhowy line, and at the same time, were promoting a new line 8½ miles long from Caerleon, through Cross Keys to a junction with the Sirhowy near Nine Mile Point. The GWR also intended to modernise the Penllwyn Tramroad (see Chapter Eight) which at this time appears to have been derelict, with part of its track torn up, at least at the northern end. All these negotiations fell through, and eventually the Monmouthshire line was taken over by the Great Western and the LNWR acquired the Sirhowy line. This was confirmed and ratified by the Act of 13th July, 1876.

New station buildings appeared between 1876 and 1878; a new wooden structure at Tredegar, a brick-built office and waiting room on the down platform at Argoed, and also new buildings at Blackwood, Tredegar Junction, Ynysddu and Nine Mile Point.

From 11th March, 1880, Sirhowy Valley trains ran into the rebuilt Newport High Street station. Prior to this, all trains used Dock Street station, running via Waterloo Junction; at Court-y-Bella they could turn left or right into Dock Street.

The section from Tredegar No. 2 signal box to south of Bedwellty was doubled *c.* 18th February, 1875, Bedwellty to Blackwood 1890/1, and the remainder on 1st September, 1891. Mr William Matthews, station master at Tredegar Junction at the time, travelled with the first train when the double line was completed.

The LNWR single line was worked by the train staff and ticket system, the staff stations being Nantybwch, Sirhowy, Tredegar, Bedwellty Pits, Hollybush, Blackwood, and Tredegar Junction. The first Hollybush station was situated about half a mile above the last station and also served the Hollybush Colliery, where the porter, amongst other duties, did all the invoicing of coal leaving the Colliery, for which he got an extra 2*s.* 3*d.* a week.

During the boom years in South Wales, extending through the second half of the 19th century up to 1914, the Sirhowy Valley presented an attractive opportunity to outside interests. The Barry Railway had built up great wealth by tapping other railways and saw here the possibility of diverting the Sirhowy coal to Barry Docks. Despite opposition from the town of Newport and the Sirhowy Valley railways which saw their prosperity threatened, the Barry Railway gained an Act in 1907 authorising a new railway from a junction with the Rhymney Railway east of Caerphilly to connect with the Sirhowy and Penllwyn lines near Nine Mile Point, and the Western Valleys branch of the GWR near Cross Keys. However a clause was inserted in Committee whereby the Barry's rates on its authorised new railways were required to be the same, irrespective of destination. As Barry Docks were further away than other competing ports, this would have meant reductions in the Barry's existing rates and made the facilities granted by Parliament unworkable. After a second attempt in 1911, the Barry's campaign was dropped the following year, and the LNW and GW railways left in undisputed possession.

A local postcard view of Argoed village High Street, c.1905 showing clearly the site of the original Tramroad. The post office and 'Jim the Barber' shop are on the right. In the background is Jediah Thomas's Butchers shop. Left foreground is the Reading Room and Library. *Author's Collection*

Blackwood High Street from a local postcard. *Author's Collection*

Chapter Four

Passenger and Freight Traffic, 1876 Onwards

Passenger Trains

The 1880 LNWR timetable was little different from the service run by the Sirhowy Railway Co., in that there were three passenger trains each way between Tredegar and Newport and about four short runs from Tredegar to Nantybwch and back. The Sunday service had ceased to run. There was a marked improvement by 1910 with seven trains to and from Newport and one additional each way between Tredegar and Nine Mile Point on Saturday mornings only. The 1915 wartime timetable had one less each way.

Passenger trains running on the branch in 1888 still had the Fay & Newall continuous brake. This consisted of a square shaft, with a universal joint between the coaches, and the guard assisted the driver in stopping at each station by turning a large wheel of about 4 ft 6 in. diameter placed vertically in his van. Failure to do this caused the driver to overrun the platform, the engines having only a hand brake with wooden blocks. On these occasions, the guard and driver would come out on to the platform and have it out! The language I am told was a mixture of English and Welsh, but for the most part unprintable.

Later, in 1900, sets of five close-coupled 4-wheelers came to Tredegar and remained in continuous use until the change over to Vestibule stock on 30th September, 1935. (During 1932 these were reduced to 4-coach units as passenger traffic diminished.) The trains were now made up of two 8-wheelers either centre vestibule or corridor, with one additional 8-wheeler for the colliers on certain trains. Vehicles in use were mainly of LNW, L&Y, and NSR origin, although from time to time they did ring the changes, and North London 4-wheeled stock was to be seen. On another occasion a rake of ex-Midland non-corridor 6-a-side coaches were running; these had the clerestory roof and gas lighting. Until roughly 1926 trains were fairly well loaded and on Saturdays two 5-coach sets were used on most trains. During Holiday Weekends the last trains out of Newport would be loaded to capacity, including front and middle vans. By 1930 the bus services were well established and took the bulk of passenger traffic, except for excursions at weekends in the summer.

The 5-coach sets, as I remember them, were made up as follows. The centre coach consisted of two Seconds and two First compartments; on each side was a coach of five Thirds and on each end a Third Brake. The partition photographs were mainly of Central Wales and the Lake District.

When the 'Vestibule Passenger Service' was introduced between Abergavenny and Merthyr in November 1932, additional services and a general speeding up of all branch line trains was made. There were now 12 trains each way, with one extra to Markham Village and Nine Mile Point. Incidentally, the fastest time between Tredegar and Newport was 55 minutes, as against the average time of 1 hr 5 min. The 4.55 pm ex-Tredegar (Except Sats) arrived at Newport at 5.50 pm; but to do this no stop was made at Bedwellty Pits, Hollybush, Pont Lawrence, or Nine Mile Point. It was intro-

SIRHOWY BRANCH—Week Days.

Up Trains.	a.m.	a.m.	a.m.	a.m.	a.m.	p.m.	p.m.	p.m.	p.m.	p.m.	p.m.
Newport (High Street.) dep	...	...	...	8 40	...	...	1 55	...	7 15	...	...
Risca ,,	Market Train, Tuesdays only.	.	.	8 57	.	.	2 12	.	7 32	.	*8 45*
Nine-Mile Point ,,		...	...	9 4	...	...	2 19	...	7 39	...	*8 52*
Ynysddu arr.		.	.	9 9	.	.	2 26	.	7 44	.	*8 57*
Tredegar Junction ,,		...	...	9 15	...	...	2 32	...	7 50	...	*9 1*
Tredegar Junction dep.		.	.	9 24	.	.	2 42	.	7 52	.	*9 2*
Blackwood ,,		...	...	9 29	...	...	2 48	...	7 57	...	*9 7*
Argoed ,,		.	.	9 35	.	.	2 55	.	8 3	.	*9 12*
Holly Bush ,,		...	...	9 40	...	...	3 3	...	8 12	...	*9 17*
Bedwellty Pits ,,		.	.	9 45	.	.	3 8	.	8 17	.	*9 23*
Tredegar arr.		...	...	9 49	...	...	3 13	...	8 21	..	*9 27*
Tredegar dep.	*6 30*	6 50	8 30	9 50	11 15	1 30	3 15	5 32	8 25	9 10	
Sirhowy ,,	*6 35*	6 55	8 35	9 55	11 20	1 35	3 20	5 36	8 30	9 15	...
Nantybwch arr.	*6 40*	7 0	8 40	10 0	11 25	1 40	—	5 40	8 35	9 20	.
Nantybwch dep.	...	...	8 45	...	11 30	2 14	...	5 52	...	9 27	Saturdays only.
Dowlais Top arr.	.	.	8 59	.	11 48	2 28	.	6 7	.	9 42	
Dowlais ,,	...	...	9 15	...	...	2 45	...	6 25	...	10 0	
Merthyr (High Street) ,,	.	.	9 27	.	12 10	2 55	.	6 35	.	10 10	
Rhymney ,,	...	...	8 59	...	11 50	2 28	...	6 14	...	9 45	
Cardiff (Rhymney) ,,	.	.	10 20		12 55	3 43	.	7 32	.	10 45	
Nantybwch dep.	*6 45*	7 12	...	10 5	...	1 47	...	5 42	8 42	...	...
Brynmawr (For Nantyglo) arr.	*7 0*	7 26	.	10 18	.	1 59	.	5 55	8 55	.	.
Abergavenny ,,	*7 37*	7 59	...	10 51	...	2 29	...	6 28	9 28	...	...

Down Trains.	a.m.	a.m.	a.m.	a.m.	p.m.	p.m.	p.m.	p.m.	p.m.	p.m.	p.m.
Abergavenny dep.	...	8 2	...	10 47	...	1 34	*2 25*	...	5 11	...	8 45
Brynmawr (For Nantyglo) dep	.	8 32	.	11 17	.	2 1	*3 8*	..	5 39	.	9 13
Nantybwch arr.	...	8 44	...	11 29	...	2 13	*3 22*	...	5 51	...	9 25
Cardiff (Rhymney) dep.	6 10	.	8 40	.	Saturdays only.	12 20	.	.	4 15	.	7 15
Rhymney ,,	6 57	...	9 47	...		1 27	...	...	5 21	...	8 27
Merthyr (High Street) ,,	6 30	.	9 25	.		1 5	.	.	5 0	.	8 0
Dowlais ,,	3 40	...	9 30	...		1 10	...	...	5 5	...	...
Dowlais Top ,,	6 56	.	9 49	.		1 30	.	.	5 26	.	8 28
Nantybwch arr.	7 10	...	10 4	...		1 46	...	...	5 41	...	8 41
Nantybwch dep.	7 12	8 50	10 10	11 33	.	2 20	*3 37*		6 0	8 50	9 35
Sirhowy arr.	7 16	8 55	10 16	11 37	...	2 25	*3 56*	4 35	6 5	8 55	9 40
Tredegar arr.	7 20	9 0	10 20	11 41	.	2 30	*3 45*	4 40	6 10	9 0	9 45
Tredegar dep.	7 21	—	...	11 43	*1 45*	...	...	4 45	*7 30*	Saturdays only.	
Bedwellty Pits ,,	7 24	.	.	11 47	*1 50*	.	Market Train, Tuesdays only.	4 50	*7 34*		.
Hollybush ,,	7 30	...	...	11 52	*2 0*	...		4 55	*7 39*		...
Argoed ,,	7 37	.	.	12 0	*2 6*	.		5 3	*7 44*		.
Blackwood ,,	7 42	...	...	12 5	*2 14*	...		5 8	*7 49*		...
Tredegar Junction ... arr.	7 46	.	.	12 9	*2 20*	.		5 13	*7 52*		.
Tredegar Junction dep.	7 47	...	...	12 10	...	...		5 25	*7 57*		...
Ynysddu ,,	7 52	.	.	12 15	.	.		5 32	*8 3*		.
Nine-Mile-Point arr.	7 58	...	...	12 21	...	...		5 41	*8 12*		...
Risca ,,	8 5	.	.	12 28	.	.		5 48	*8 20*		.
Bassalleg ,,	8 14	...	...	12 37	...	...	...	5 57	...	...	...
Newport (High Street.) ,,	8 22	.	.	12 45	.	.	.	6 5	.		.

Passenger Timetable for June 1884.

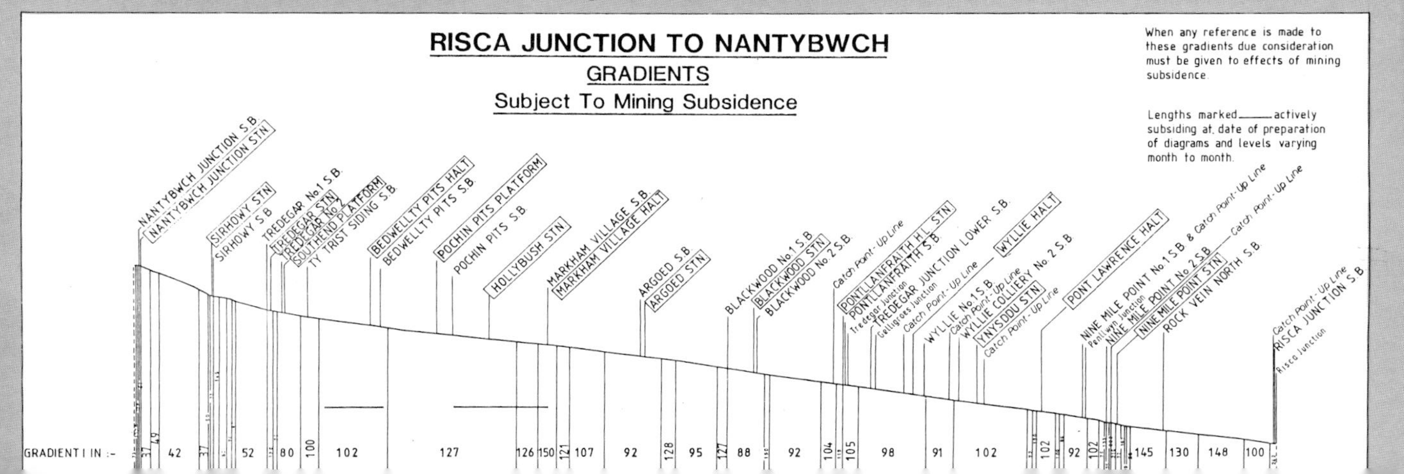

duced to give a fairly fast connection for passengers to London at Newport and was favoured by Tredegar Iron & Coal Company's officials at Tredegar and Markham. For a time the 2.09 pm ex-Tredegar and the 9. 05 pm ex-Newport did not stop at Risca, unless prior notice was given, and of course, no trains stopped at Bassaleg Junction unless notice was given, either to station staff or to the train guard, although according to the Working Timetable of 1880 down passenger trains stopped there at that time.

Markham Village station did not come into service until 1917 but there was a platform on the up side from about 1892 to cater for the Bargoed Coal Company's Abernant Colliery workmen. (The Colliery, which was closed about 1932, was just south of the platform.) During the sinking of Markham Colliery in 1910, another platform was erected on the down side, but the station was not used for passenger traffic until 1st February, 1917. Markham Colliery closed in 1987 and Oakdale Colliery in 1989, thus ending an era in coal mining in the Sirhowy Valley extending to well over 200 years. Both collieries were situated on Hall's Road which has now been closed. The Markham colliers used the Sirhowy line for getting to and from work until the buses took over after the war, although there were a few workmen's trains running under contract until the branch closed.

One train which stood the test of time was the 4.20 am Newport–Tredegar Passenger and Mails (originally 4.30 am from Newport). Vehicles for this train – two passenger vans and a Third Brake – were taken down at the rear of the 7.52 pm Tredegar to Newport train the night before. The 'Mail' was worked by the engine of a mineral train running from Tredegar in the early hours of the morning to Nine Mile Point, and then running light from there to Newport arriving at 4.00 am. Later, coaching stock for working the mail ran from Tredegar, arriving Newport at 3.45 am, but by 1955 the stock used came from the Newport area, so no empty stock was required from Tredegar. An extract from the LMS monthly staff publication *On Time* for October 1936, shows that the Sirhowy Valley staff could rise to the occasion when required:

> Off the beaten track, on secondary and branch lines the 'On time' spirit flourishes just as strongly as with the most important express passenger and freight trains on the main lines. Down in the mountain valleys of South and Central Wales, for instance, there are few opportunities for spectacular performance, but here are two cases where smart operating pleased the public. Going through his train, (7.12 am Nantybwch–Newport) as it left Nantybwch 7 mins late (through waiting connection with a train running late from the North) Guard Tom Michael (Tredegar) discovered that three passengers held tickets for the GW line via Pontllanfraith, where the connection might be missed. From Nantybwch the train makes seven calls up to Pontllanfraith, but Guard Michael explained the position to Driver R.L. Evans and Fireman J. Howells (Abergavenny) with the result that the 7 mins late start was recovered and the connection at Pontllanfraith duly made.
>
> On the same day the same three men did a similarly smart piece of work with the 11.08 am Nantybwch to Newport, making up 7 mins between Tredegar and Newport and thus enabling passengers to make important main line connections at the latter place.

The Sirhowy branch was absorbed into the Western Region in 1948–49, and controlled from Newport as from 1st January, 1951. The year 1955 may be regarded as the commencement of a gradual decline in the service generally; trains were now running to Risca only, with a connection for Newport, and a change at Risca in the reverse direction. There were a few exceptions – the 6.00 pm from Nantybwch and the 7.52 pm from Tredegar were through to Newport, and the 4.20 am Passenger and Mails still ran to Tredegar; also the 7.37 pm and 10.00 pm (Sats only) through from Newport to Nantybwch. The train would consist of one coach and pannier tank, working as a motor train.

The same year, 1955, was also the year when a little light comedy was introduced into the timetable folder – the letter B opposite Nine Mile Point on the timetable informed the traveller that Nine Mile Point was also the station for Upper Machen (1½ miles). It seems unlikely that many passengers made this desolate journey over Machen Mountain, (1,193 ft). The entry was not included in subsequent issues!

Excursion Traffic

Up to 1914 the excursion traffic was concentrated on the north; Hereford, Shrewsbury, Liverpool, Manchester, Blackpool, Glasgow and Edinburgh. These trips centred on Easter, Whitsun, and August and during these weekends all coal traffic ceased and only perishable goods ran. As many signal boxes as possible were opened to shorten the sections and trains were double-headed, as far as the locomotive department would allow. There were always coaches with the white cross on the solebar, indicating that they were not completely finished and must be returned to Crewe or Wolverton immediately after use. On occasions the main line engine would come down the valley to work these trains and I remember seeing LNWR 4–6–0 No. 88 *Czar of Russia* at Argoed station on an up excursion to Blackpool somewhere around 1922. It was not the general practice to use these engines, and as a rule two of the 'Coal' tanks or an 0–8–0 tender engine would head the train. The main line engines would then take the train forward from Abergavenny, Brecon Road. Family Saloons were very popular on the MT & A District, used chiefly by the clubs.

Excursion traffic commenced again about 1920, and by 1930 the pattern had changed considerably. Trips were now running to Barry Island at Easter, Whitsun and August, and also every Saturday from May to September. Traffic to the North consisted of specials to Murrayfield and to Belfast via Heysham. The Murrayfield trains would have the unique combination of an 0–8–4T and 0–8–0 tender engine at the head of the train. These trains would have ten modern 8-wheelers and often included a dining car. As many as five specials would run to Barry Island on Saturdays in the summer. Starting from Nantybwch, the first two would be through to Blackwood, then Pontllanfraith, which was their last stop. The remainder would stop at all stations, the last train consisting of anything they could lay their hands on at Tredegar; either 4-, 6- or 8-wheelers and a variety of companies including ex-LNW, L&Y, NSR, Midland, North London and even an ex-M &GN coach. These trains were hauled by the 0–8–0 tender engines ('G1'

–'G2') and on odd occasions by the Hughes 2–6–0 tender engines. Trains would leave the Sirhowy Line at Pontllanfraith, through Bird-in-Hand Junction, and over Walnut Tree Viaduct on to the former Barry Railway system.

Before 1935, 4- and 6-wheel LNW coaches were running on the Barry Island trains; on 9th September, 1933 the Half-Day Excursion was made up of thirteen 4-wheelers and one 6-wheel Brake Third – the fare from Tredegar was 3*s.* and 2*s.* 6*d.* from Blackwood. On 14th August, 1937 ex-MR 0–6–0 No. 4347 headed a Barry Island excursion consisting of seven 8-wheel Clerestory ex-MR coaches; six-a-side, non-corridor, with gas lighting. These had the first class compartments marked 3rd, but were not altered inside except for the removal of the anti-macassars. A very comfortable 'third class' ride!

When the engine went through, a GW pilotman would be picked up at Ystrad South. The crew booked off at Barry Island, where they would remain until return and the engine was shedded at Barry. If the locomotive department at Tredegar was short of staff or engines, the train would be taken forward from Ystrad South by GW or ex-Rhymney 0–6–2 side tanks. Football specials to Pontypridd and Cardiff took the same route to Ystrad South, but some Cardiff trains were routed via Nine Mile Point, Park Junction, Ebbw Junction, and on to the GW main line to Cardiff (Queen Street) station, where I once recorded an approximate speed of 52 mph by 0–8–0 No. 8899.

On the Royal Gwent Hospital Carnival Day at Newport in early August, all trains would be strengthened to the maximum load for the Sirhowy branch. The trains invariably lost time on their return journey up the Valley; due to their length, they had to pull up twice at many of the stations. In one instance the crossing gates at Pontllanfraith suffered, as a reliefman replaced the gates one night on to the headstock of the last vehicle of a return excursion which had not quite cleared the gates. The result was disastrous; the gate was completely severed from the corner post!

There were also Day Excursions to Bristol and the South, Weston-super-Mare and London, but these were run by the ordinary train service, with a change at Newport. School children specials from roughly 1950 were worked by Western Region coaches and engines; these would be worked up the Valley early in the morning as 'empty stock' by ex-GW 0–6–2 side tanks. Occasionally GW Aberdare to London and Bristol Excursions were run via Sirhowy Junction and Nine Mile Point. Shrewsbury Flower Show specials ran via Abergavenny and Hereford. From 1958 Barry Island trains were worked by Western Region, hauled by the ex-GW 0–6–2 side tanks which came from either Radyr or Ebbw Junction sheds. Many specials came up the valley during the 1940 evacuation of the Greater London area, mainly of GW stock, but SR green was to be seen at times.

Workmen's Trains

There was an extensive colliers' train service not shown in the Public timetable. These trains ran between Nantybwch, Tredegar, Markham Village and Nine Mile Point. The coaches were stored at Nantybwch, Rhoswen Sidings (Argoed) and Nine Mile Point. A colliers' train ran for many years to and from Pochin Pits, made up of eighteen mixed 4- and 6-wheelers (twenty on occasions) headed by one of the 0–6–2 'Coal' tank engines. During the 1914–18 period there were in all 17 colliers' trains in operation over the 24 hours. These trains were worked by the goods guards who shared mixed duties with the mineral traffic. Incidentally, the Tredegar Iron & Coal Company ran their own workmen's train service from the top of Tredegar Yard to their Whitworth and Ty-Trist Collieries. These ran for the morning, afternoon and night shifts, and were hauled by their own 0–6–0 saddle tank engines. The railway company's trains were not allowed to enter the Tredegar Company's Yard during the running of their own workman's service. Up to about 1926 almost all colliers from the Tredegar and Blackwood areas travelled by train, if the distance was more than they were prepared to walk. My father was at Markham Village at the time, where they were handling more than a thousand colliers to the Markham and Abernant collieries.

The colliers' train service worked very smoothly as a rule; but you cannot convey this number each day without some disruption of service occasionly. Having worked amongst the colliers all his life, my father prided himself on his relationship with them; but it did require tact at times when, for instance, a breakdown occurred and the men were kept waiting – they didn't mind how they got home, as long as they got home! In one instance, the engine failed on an up colliers' train one afternoon, leaving about 400 men stranded, all from the Tredegar and Sirhowy area. An up passenger train was due just before the colliers' train, but in those days, even on the Sirhowy Line trains were reasonably loaded and one had to satisfy both ordinary passengers and colliers. It was solved by packing the workmen into both front and rear vans of the passenger train, the remainder filling the compartments – on the strict understanding that they stood up, and did not soil the seats. My father spoke to Charlie Carter who was station master at Bedwellty Pits at the time, and he confirmed that the men were standing when the train passed there. I think they obeyed principally because my father gave in to them on other points, and always allowed 2–3 minutes late start for running colliers. (The colliers were covered in coal dust from head to foot on leaving their work, and for this reason their own coaches had slatted seats.)

There were always those trying to get a free ride, especially on the return afternoon shift during darkness, when they would board the train on the 'off' side to the platform. This also occurred in the winter mornings. On the arrival of the 'down colliers' one morning about 15 got out on the wrong side, only to be caught by three LNWR detectives posing as platelayers!

The arrival of the early morning colliers' at Pochin Platform was a sight to see – almost everyone was clear of the train by the time it had come to a halt, and one or two even professed to 'call their lamps' before the train came to a stand. As far as I know, no one was killed, but there were a few broken legs over the years.

Still on colliers' trains, I believe the funniest story of them all concerns the train serving the morning shift at Pochin and a well-known LNWR passenger guard at the time. The men were not allowed to take cigarettes, matches, etc.

TRAIN SERVICE

NANTYBWCH, SIRHOWY AND NEWPORT (Weekdays only)

	Station																SO	SX					SO	SX	SX	SO	
			a.m.	a.m.	a.m.	a.m	a.m.	a.m.		a.m.	p.m.	p.m.	p.m.		p.m.	p.m.		p.m.	p.m.	p.m.	p.m.	p.m.	p.m.	p.m.	p.m.	p.m.	p.m.	
	Nantybwch	dep.	...	7 12	8 24	8 48	9 21	9 48	...	11 8	12 55	2 0	2 53	...	...	...	...	...	...	5 12	5 55	7 35	8 25	9 10	9 30	10 5	10 10	...
	Sirhowy	,,	...	7 17	8 29	8 52	9 28	9 52	...	11 12	1 0	2 4	2 57	...	...	...	...	4 42	...	5 16	5 59	7 41	8 30	9 15	9 35	10 9	10 14	...
	Tredegar	arr.	...	7 20	8 33	8 56	9 32	9 56	...	11 16	1 4	2 8	3 1	...	...	...	...	4 45	...	5 23	6 3	7 48	8 33	9 18	9 43	10 13	10 18	...
	Tredegar	dep.	5 45	7 22	8 35	...	...	9 58	...	11 18	1 10	2 9	...	...	4 15	...	...	4 50	4 55	...	6 5	7 52	...	9 25	9 44	10 14	10 22	...
	Bedwellty Pits	,,	5 49	7 26	8 39	...	...	10 3	...	11 23	1 15	2 12	...	...	4 18	...	...	4 55		...	6 10	7 57	...	9 30	9 48	10 20	10 27	...
	Holly Bush	,,	5 56	7 31	8 44	...	...	10 8	...	11 28	1 20	2 17	...	...	4 23	...	...	5 0	...	...	6 15	8 3	...	9 35	9 53	10 28	10 32	...
	Markham Village Halt	,,	5 59	7 34	8 47	...	...	10 11	...	11 32	1 24	2 20	...	...	4 27	...	...	5 4	5 4	...	6 18	8 7	...	9 40	9 58	10 33	10 37	...
	Argoed	,,	6 4	7 38	8 51	...	...	10 16	...	11 37	1 28	2 25	...	...	4 32	...	...	5 8	5 8	...	6 23	8 12	...	9 46	10 4	...	10 43	...
	Blackwood	,,	6 9	7 44	8 56	...	...	10 21	...	11 43	1 34	2 30	...	...	4 36	...	...	5 14	5 14	...	6 29	8 18	...	9 52	10 9	...	10 49	...
	Pontllanfraith	arr.	6 14	7 49	9 1	...	...	10 25	...	11 47	1 39	2 35	...	...	4 41	...	...	5 18	5 18	...	6 33	8 22	...	9 56	10 14	...	10 53	...
	Pontllanfraith	dep.	6 15	7 50	9 3	...	...	10 26	...	11 48	1 40	2 37	...	...	4 42	...	...	5 19	5 19	...	6 34	8 23	...	9 58	10 17	...	10 55	...
	Wyllie Halt	,,	6 18	7 53	9 6	...	...	10 29	...	11 51	1 43	2 41	...	...	4 45	...	...	5 22	...	...	6 38	8 26	...	10 1	10 21	...	10 58	...
	Ynysddu	,,	6 20	7 55	9 8	...	...	10 31	...	11 53	1 46	2 43	...	...	4 46	...	...	5 24	5 24	...	6 40	8 28	...	10 4	10 26	...	11 0	...
	Pont Lawrence	,,	6 23	7 59	9 11	...	...	10 35	...	11 57	1 49	2 46	...	...	4 49	...	...	5 27	...	...	6 44	8 32	...	10 9	10 29	...	11 3	...
	Nine-Mile-Point	,,	6 27	8 4	9 15	...	...	10 40	...	12 3	1 53	2 51	...	...	4 53	...	...	5 32	...	...	6 50	8 37	...	10 14	10 33	...	11 6	...
G.W.R.	Risca	,,	6 33	8 11	9 21	...	...	10 46	...	12 10	2 0	C	...	...	5 1	5 9	...	5 37	5 33	...	6 56	8 42	...	10 19	...	...	...	...
G.W.R.	Bassaleg Junction	,,	AB	AB	AB	...	...	AB	...	AB	AB	AB	...	...	...	5 21	...	AB	AB	...	AB	AB	...	AB	...	...	...	...
G.W.R.	Newport	arr.	6 49	8 27	9 37	...	...	10 58	...	12 23	2 16	3 20	...	...	...	5 29	...	5 55	5 50	...	7 10	9 0	...	10 37	...	...	...	...
G.W.R.	Cardiff (General)	,,	7 49	8 48	10 14	...	...	11 18	...	12 56	2 36	3 42	...	...	...	5 51	...	6 19	6 19	...	7 48	9X25	...	12 14	...	...	...	...

	Station																						SO	SX	SO	
			a.m.	a.m.	a.m.	a.m.	a.m.	a.m.		a.m.	p.m.	a.m.	p.m.		p.m.	p.m.	p.m.	p.m.	p.m.	p.m.	p.m.	p.m.	p.m.	p.m.	p.m.	p.m.	
G.W.R.	Cardiff (General)	dep.	...	...	...	...	6 55	8 30	...	10 15	...	11 50	12 35	...	2 40	3 45	4 35	...	...	...	7 0	...	8 21	9 30	10 30	10 30	...
G.W.R.	Newport	,,	4 30	...	...	...	7 22	8 50	...	10 38	...	12 15	1 10	...	3 10	4 8	4 59	...	...	...	7 35	...	9 5	10 0	10 55	11 12	...
G.W.R.	Bassaleg Junction	,,	...	...	...	...	BB	BB	...	BB	...	BB	BB	...	BB	BB	5 6	...	...	...	BB	...	BB	BB	BB	BB	...
G.W.R.	Risca	,,	4 47	...	...	...	7 40	9 5	...	10 53	...	12 30	1 26	...	3 26	4 22	5 17	5 20	...	...	7 52	...	D	10 17	E	11 28	...
	Nine-Mile-Point	,,	4 54	...	...	...	7 47	9 11	...	10 59	...	12 36	1 32	...	3 32	4 28	...	5 25	...	...	7 58	...	9 29	10 23	11 14	11 34	...
	Pont Lawrence	,,	...	...	...	...	7 51	9 14	...	11 3	...	12 39	1 35	...	3 35	...	...	5 28	...	...	8 1	...	9 33	10 27	11 17	11 38	...
	Ynysddu	,,	5 1	...	...	...	7 56	9 18	...	11 8	...	12 44	1 39	...	3 39	4 34	...	5 32	...	...	8 5	...	9 37	10 31	11 21	11 42	...
	Wyllie Halt	,,	...	...	...	...	7 58	9 20	...	11 10	...	12 47	1 41	...	3 42	4 37	...	5 35	...	...	8 7	...	9 39	10 33	11 23	11 44	...
	Pontllanfraith	arr.	5 6	...	...	...	8 1	9 23	...	11 14	...	12 52	1 44	...	3 45	4 41	...	5 38	...	...	8 10	...	9 43	10 37	11 27	11 47	...
	Pontllanfraith	dep.	5 8	...	...	...	8 9	9 25	...	11 15	...	12 53	1 46	...	3 46	4 42	...	5 39	...	...	8 12	...	9 44	10 38	11 28	11 48	...
	Blackwood	,,	5 14	...	...	...	8 18	9 31	...	11 19	...	12 57	1 53	...	3 53	4 46	...	5 43	...	...	8 18	...	9 50	10 42	11 33	11 53	...
	Argoed	,,	...	...	...	...	8 23	9 36	...	11 25	...	1 4	1 58	...	3 58	4 52	...	5 51	...	...	8 23	...	9 55	10 49	11 42	11 58	...
	Markham Village Halt	,,	...	...	...	...	8 33	9 44	...	11 32	...	1 10	2 6	...	4 6	4 59	...	5 56	...	...	8 32	...	10 6	10 57	11 47	12 7	...
	Holly Bush	,,	...	...	...	...	8 37	9 48	...	11 37	...	1 14	2 10	...	4 10	5 3	...	6 0	...	...	8 37	...	10 10	11 2	11 51	12 11	...
	Bedwellty Pits	,,	...	...	...	...	8 42	9 55	...	11 42	...	1 21	2 15	...	4 15	5 8	...	6 5	...	...	8 42	...	10 18	11 8	11 56	12 18	...
	Tredegar	arr.	5 34	...	...	...	8 47	10 3	...	11 47	...	1 27	2 20	...	4 20	5 14	...	6 11	...	...	8 47	...	10 24	11 15	12 2	12 24	...
	Tredegar	dep.	...	6 50	8 0	8 25	9 25	10 27	...	...	12 3	1 32	2 25	...	4 30	5 15	...	6 12	7 15	8 5	8 50	9 35	10 30	11 18	12 4	12 28	...
	Sirhowy	,,	...	6 53	8 3	8 28	9 28	10 32	...	...	12 6	1 35	2 28	...	4 33	5 18	...	6 15	7 18	8 8	8 58	9 38	10 33	11 21	12 7	12 31	...
	Nantybwch	arr.	...	7 1	8 10	8 40	9 35	10 37	...	...	12 13	1 42	2 36	...	4 40	5 25	...	...	7 25	8 17	9 5	9 47	10 40	...	...	...	...

AB—Calls at Bassaleg Junction to set down from Sirhowy line stations on notice being given by the passenger to the guard. BB—Calls at Bassaleg Junction when required to pick up passengers for Sirhowy line stations on notice being given at the station.

C—Calls at Risca to set down if required, on notice being given to the guard at Nine-Mile-Point.

D—Calls at Risca to pick up if required.

E—Calls at Risca to pick up passengers for the Sirhowy line on notice being given at the station.

SX—Saturdays excepted. SO—Saturdays only.

X—9.49 p.m. on Saturdays.

LMS Pocket timetable for the Sirhowy Valley, September 1936.

down the pit, but in order that they could enjoy their smoke on the journey, there was a gentlemen's agreement between them that these items could be left on the rack in the compartments of the coaches. Each collier had his tin on the rack where he would sit, and as the same stock was used for the return journey, the system worked extremely well – that is until one afternoon, when the men returned from their day shift and found their tobacco tins, cigarettes etc, switched around from one end of the train to the other, mixing them all up in the process! Pandemonium reigned when this was found out and it took 20 minutes to settle the matter and start for Tredegar.

There were still a few workmen's trains running in 1957–58 under contract with the NCB between Nantybwch and Nine Mile Point and back but some of these were 'Q' trains (i.e. run as required) as the number of men carried had decreased considerably by then. Around 1942 another workmen's service started to run, and this was to the Northern Aluminium Company (now named Alcan Industries Ltd) at Rogerstone. Trains were run to cover the three shifts and were available also to the public who could get a connection for Newport by changing at Rogerstone. The service ran for about 12 years. Colliery platforms were in use at South End, (Tredegar) Pochin and Abernant. Coal traffic from Markham Colliery went over Hall's Road (later GW and BR) until the Colliery closed in 1987. The Great Western cleared traffic from Wyllie and Nine Mile Point collieries via Newport using pannier tanks or the 2–8–0 tank engines. During World War I the LNW worked some coal from Nine Mile Point northwards via Tredegar and Abergavenny Junction.

The following collieries were served by the Workmen's Trains:

Graham Navigation, Sirhowy
Whitworth
Ty-Trist
Bedwellty Pits
Pochin
Hollybush
Markham
Abernant
Budds Rock Colliery, Blackwood
Wyllie
Nine Mile Point

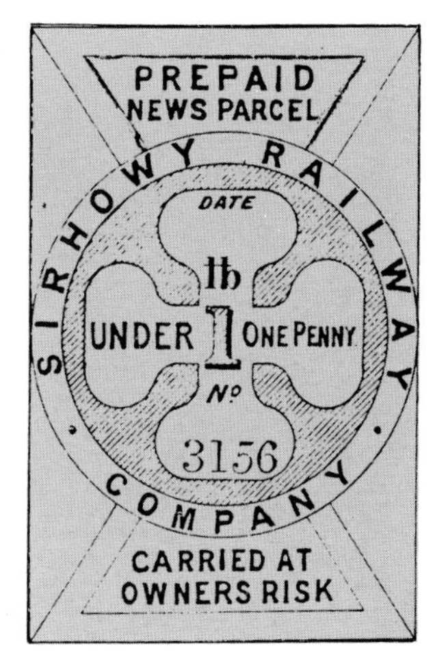

A sample of Prepaid News Parcel stamps issued by the Company:
Design 1868. 44 × 68 mm in sheets; 4 rows of 3 stamps.
1d. black on white, Perf 10
2d. black on rose, Perf 10
3d. black on blue, Perf 10

The last passenger train to leave Tredegar on 11th June, 1960, with as usual a crowd to see it off! *Author*

A train of 'empties' seen here on the former Hall's Road (GWR) in 1980. The train is proceeding to Markham Colliery having just passed over the crossing gates at Court-y-bella, near Argoed. *Courtesy Cyril Jones*

Mineral and Goods Traffic

Those twin-kings of the earth, Iron and Coal, were the main sources of revenue in the Sirhowy Valley. Coal came from the many collieries in the Tredegar area and down the valley to Nine Mile Point. Iron was produced by the Tredegar Iron & Coal Company, and by Messrs Whiteheads, who came to Tredegar in 1903. Goods sheds were situated at Sirhowy and Blackwood, with smaller ones at Argoed and Ynysddu Lower. Part of the shed at Blackwood and Argoed was rented for many years to Messrs Crawford Biscuits. Station-to-station goods traffic was good until approximately 1925 when road competition reduced the volume considerably.

From the Late J.M. Dunn's *Reflections on a Railway Career*:

> The traffic figures for a small place like Tredegar were somewhat surprising, as from 60 to 62 passenger and colliers' trains were dealt with in the course of 24 hours. During the month of March 1928 no less than 8,559 wagons passed in and out the Tredegar Iron & Coal Co's Yard. During the same month the total number of wagons moved on the Sirhowy line was 33,560.

As traffic increased it was found necessary to marshal the down coal trains into some formation before going forward to Nine Mile Point or Ystrad South, and to accomplish this Rhoswen Sidings and signal box came into service about August 1912. The signal box was worked as required by Argoed signalmen, being so shown from 15th December, 1945 in the WTT. In 'North Western' days horsebox specials ran to Blackwood for the Bedwellty Show, held on the first Monday in September. An additional portable Booking Office (Webb Hut) was placed at the north end of the station for passengers going in the Newport direction. Passenger trains were duplicated as required.

Closure

The passenger service between Risca and Nantybwch was withdrawn on 13th June, 1960. As there was no Sunday service, the last trains ran on Saturday 11th June, 1960. The 6.33 pm from Risca to Tredegar was extended to Nantybwch, and left there at 7.52 pm. Going up from Tredegar to Nantybwch, the train engine, No. 7811, was placed in the rear and another engine, which had worked the 3.33 pm ex-Risca, headed the train, now increased to four coaches. On the return journey from Nantybwch, both engines were in front.

Freight traffic ceased as follows:

Nantybwch–Sirhowy	closed	13th June, 1960
Sirhowy–Tredegar	"	4th November, 1963
Tredegar–Pontllanfraith	"	30th April, 1969
Tredegar–Risca	"	4th May, 1970

but very few trains ran after passenger services ceased. Nine Mile Point Colliery closed in July 1964 and Wyllie Colliery in March 1968. The lower part of the valley was finally closed to colliery traffic in April 1970. Little remains now of the railway; just one or two buildings – the station building at Tredegar and the station master's house at Hollybush. Elsewhere there are traces of platform positions as at Argoed and Blackwood. At Pochin and Markham the NCB have spread massive tips over the area.

All those familiar sounds – the shrill 'North Western' whistle, and the persistent slipping of an 0–8–0 bringing up 59 'empties' and the Van – have gone for ever.

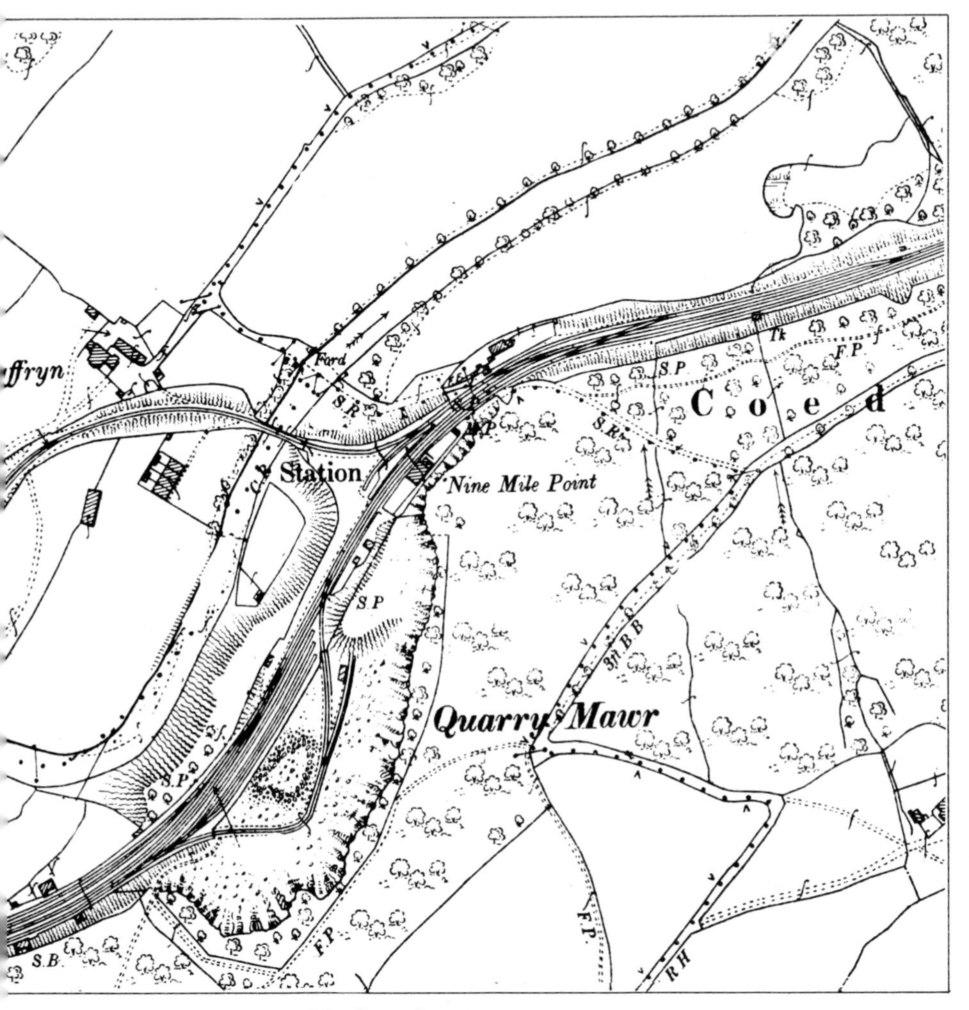

Nine Mile Point station and Penllwyn Junction.

Reproduced from the 1904, 25" Ordnance Survey Map

Risca Junction station seen between 1886 and 1910, prior to the conversion to four platforms (with island platform in the middle). A GWR coal train is seen approaching from Aberbeeg and the original Risca long Viaduct towards Nantybauch curves sharply to the left behind the small cottage. Note the well kept signal box garden.
Author

A view in the Ebbw Valley looking from the Monmouthshire canal across towards Risca, c.1890. Original course of the Sirhowy line is seen in the background, the GWR branch to Nine Mile Point (and the LNWR Sirhowy) *centre*, and the GWR Western Valleys line is in the foreground.
Author

Nine Mile Point No. 1 signal box looking north in September 1969. The junction is called Penllwyn, with the track on the extreme right being the weighing machine road and extended almost to Nine Mile Point station. *R.H. Marrows*

A good general view of Burnyeat Brown & Co (Coronation) colliery at Nine Mile Point. *Author*

A view in the rain of Nine Mile Point, LNWR station facing Tredegar on 12th July, 1958. *R.M. Casserley*

This photograph is of poor quality, but an early view of Port Lawrence station looking south east towards Newport. *Courtesy Ray Potter*

A track view of Ynysddu station looking south towards Newport on 12th July, 1958.
R.M. Casserley

The sweeping wooden platforms of Wyllie station looking south on the rainy day of 12th July, 1958 with the colliery to the right of the line in the left background.
R.M. Casserley

A view of GWR 0–6–0PT, No. 3747 coming out Wyllie colliery past No.1 box on 11th July, 1958, into Wyllie station. *H.C. Casserley*

A last look at Wyllie station/halt, this time looking north, again on the rainy day of 12th July, 1958. *H.C. Casserley*

This view is of Wyllie colliery just after opening showing clearly the acutely curved trackwork within the complex. *Author*

Tredegar Junction Lower signal box (looking north) showing the 'up' home signals and the GWR Sirhowy Junction distant signal on 16th April, 1963. *R.H. Marrows*

The ex-GWR, Bird in Hand West Junction (looking east from the GWR line) showing the home signals for the main line (*left*) and the LMS branch to the Sirhowy Valley line on the right. The left distant signal is for the GWR Pontllanfraith station box and right is the fixed distant for the LMS crossing box. *R.H. Marrows*

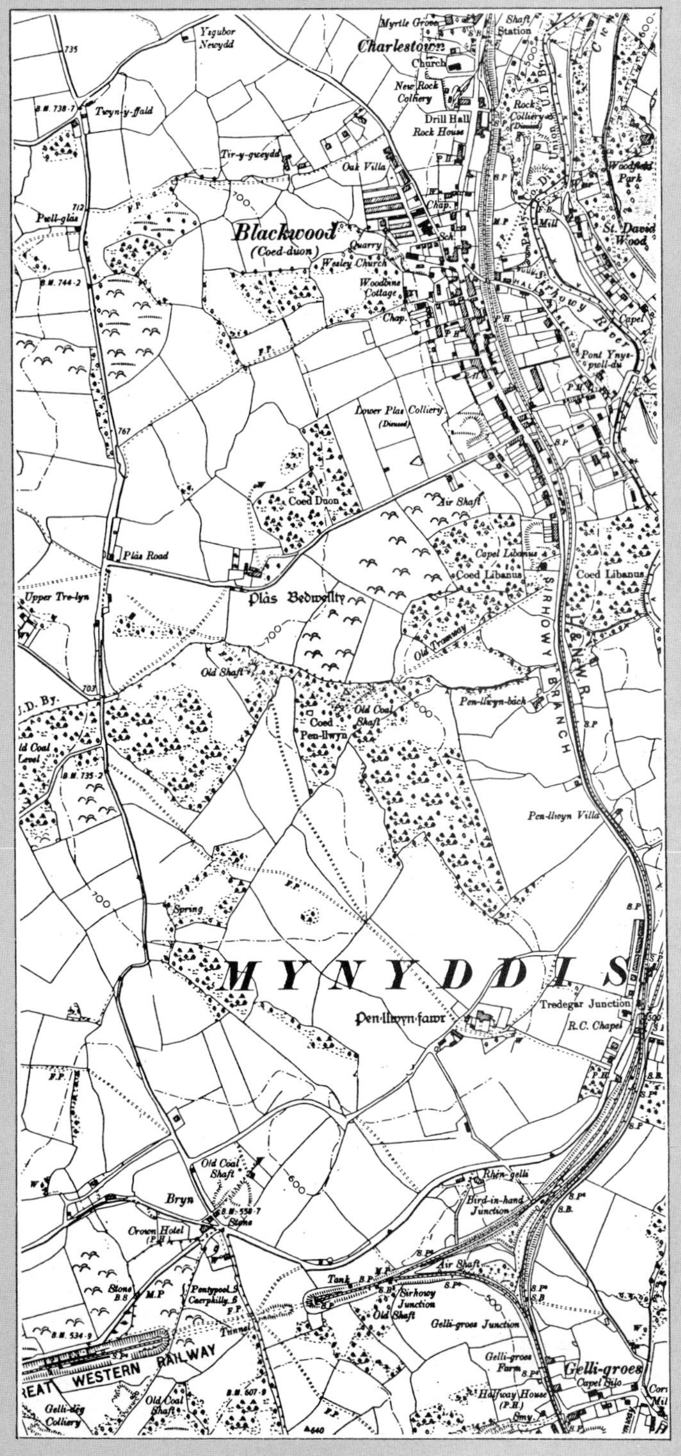

Blackwood station (*top*) and the triangular junction (Bird-in-Hand) with the Sirhowy Valley line going over the top at Tredegar Junction.

Reduced and reproduced from the 1904, 6" Ordnance Survey Map

The LNWR bridge crossing over the Great Western metals at Pontllanfraith, looking west in February 1966. *R.H. Marrows*

Sirhowy Junction as seen on 17th May, 1964. The lines to the left lead to Pontypool Road and those to the right are for Newport via Tredegar Junction Lower. *Michael Hale*

An early view in 1920 of Pontllanfraith High Level showing the station buildings and signal box. *Author*

Looking north towards Pontllanfraith LNW station with the machine Rd and office in the middle distance; the Bird-in-Hand Public House is on the right. *R.H. Marrows*

Pontllanfraith station in LNWR days. Note the covered van in Bryn siding.
C.H. Forrester

Pontllanfraith LNW station seen from the road. The roof was blown off by a gas explosion on 20th October, 1952. *British Rail*

A LNWR 'Coal' tank on an up train seen here at Pontllanfraith. *Derek Chaplin*

A last look at Pontllanfraith station, this time in the down direction on 10th July, 1958. *H.C. Casserley*

Blackwood station showing both the up and down platforms in the 1920's. The top photograph is looking south, with the connection to New Rock Colliery visible, the bottom picture is looking north. *(Both) Lens of Sutton*

Two more views of Blackwood station looking north. The top photograph was captured in LNWR days with station staff posed for their picture whilst the lower photograph taken on 11th July, 1959 shows the station in BR(WR) days. The grounded coach body seen in the top picture was the station master's office later replaced by a 'Webb Hut'. *Lens of Sutton and H.C. Casserley*

The sturdy wooden construction of the winding gear at the pit head of Budd's Rock Colliery, Blackwood. *Author*

Auto train with coach W207W leading, seen here at Blackwood station, just before closure. *Courtesy Miss Bisgrove*

The 10.38 am Newport to Nantybwch service seen here at Blackwood station on 29th July, 1935. The close-coupled 4-coach set is being hauled by a coal side-tank No. 7712. *Author's Collection*

A view from the hilltop of Argoed railway station and High Street, looking south. The down platform buildings were built in 1878; note the staggered platform layout. The siding behind the platform on the right was the original line to Cwm Creeich Colliery.
Author's Collection

The 3.10 pm Newport to Nantybwch service with a good variety of coaching stock, the last coach being a colliers' coach. This scene was captured on 11th August, 1936; 'Coal' tank No. 7814 was scrapped the following December. *Author's Collection*

The special train bringing the VIPs (via Hall's Road GWR) in 1907 to the ceremony of 'cutting the first sod' at Oakdale Colliery. *Author's Collection*

Cutting of the first sod by Miss Markham at Oakdale Colliery site in 1907. It does seem to be a 'Ladies' VIP gathering! *Author's Collection*

Llanover Colliery, Bargoed Coal Company. *Author's Collection*

A view of Oakdale Colliery during its construction. This was situated on Hall's Road (GWR). Note the wagon loading screens on the extreme right. *Author's Collection*

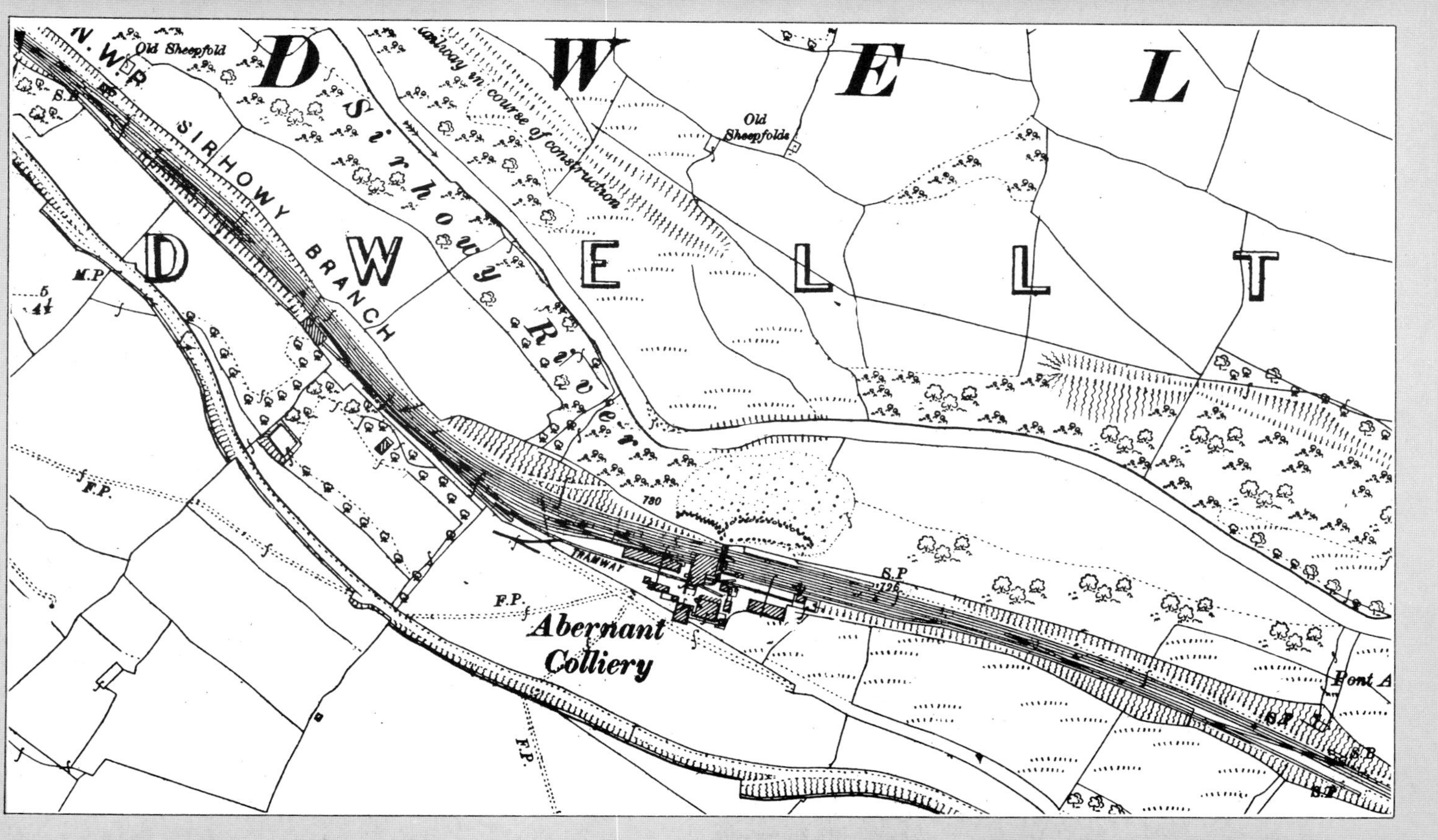

Abernant Colliery.

Reduced and reproduced from the 1904, 25″ Ordnance Survey Map

Abernant Colliery full of Bargoed P.O. wagons. The scene is looking south.
Courtesy C.J.R. Wilson

Markham Colliery (Hall's Road GWR). *Author's Collection*

Markham Village signal box as seen from the colliers halt up platform, looking north.
Gerald Davies

A busy scene at Holly Bush station around 1908, with trains due in both directions. Note the colliery behind the ornate footbridge; view looking north.
Author's Collection

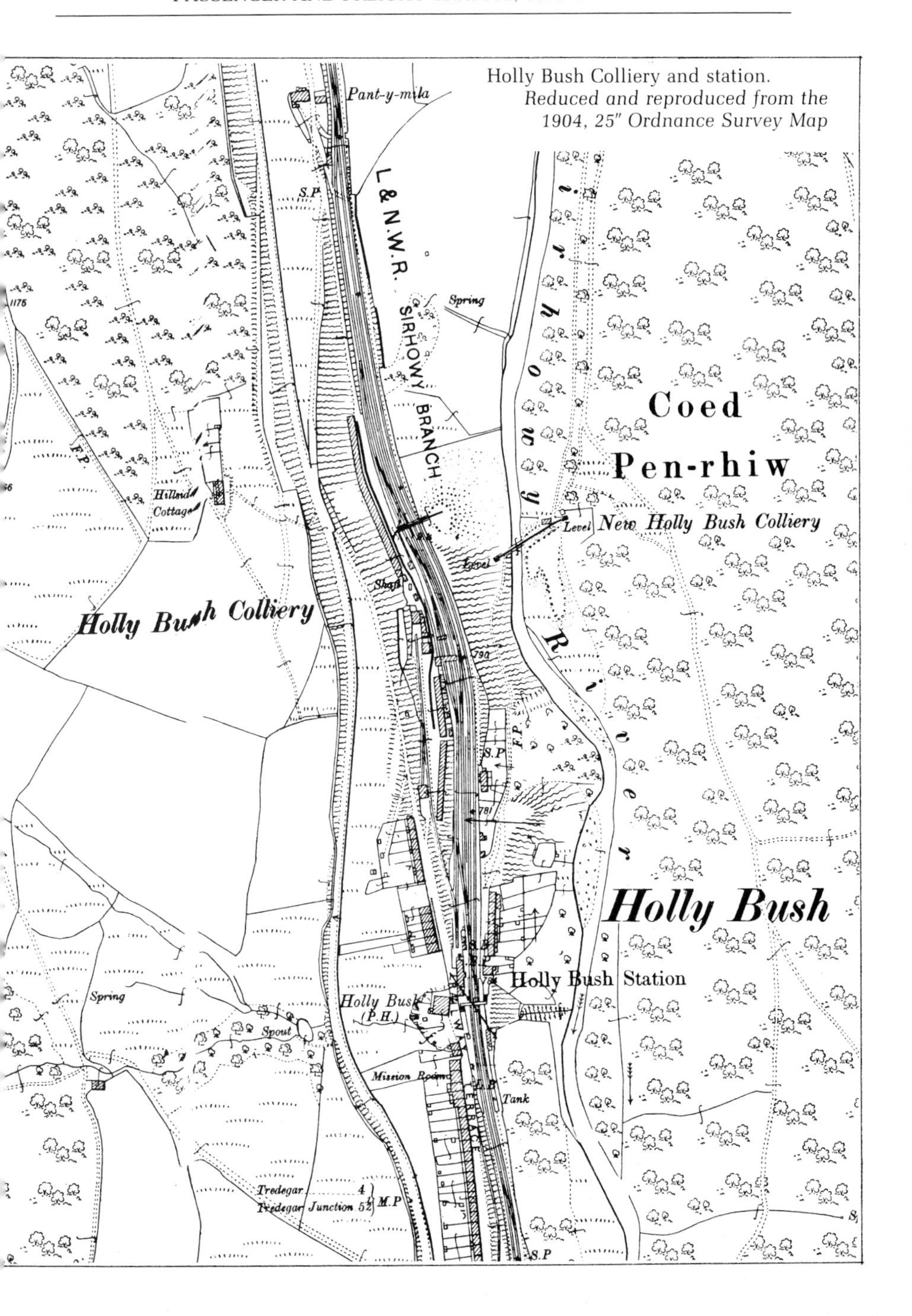

Holly Bush Colliery and station. *Reduced and reproduced from the 1904, 25″ Ordnance Survey Map*

A further pre-grouping view of Holly Bush station down platform with a member of the station staff at attention for the camera! This view shows more detail of the footbridge and the platform built on the side of a steep slope. *Author's Collection*

A good view of the Colliery wagons waiting to go under the screens for filling; looking south. Note the Barry Railway wagons. *C.J.R. Wilson*

Locomotive No. 1005 just about to start with a thirteen-coach well-packed colliers' train at Pochin Pits Colliery platform. The engine was renumbered 7705 by the LMS. (Built October 1889 and withdrawn November 1916.) *Courtesy Peter Jones*

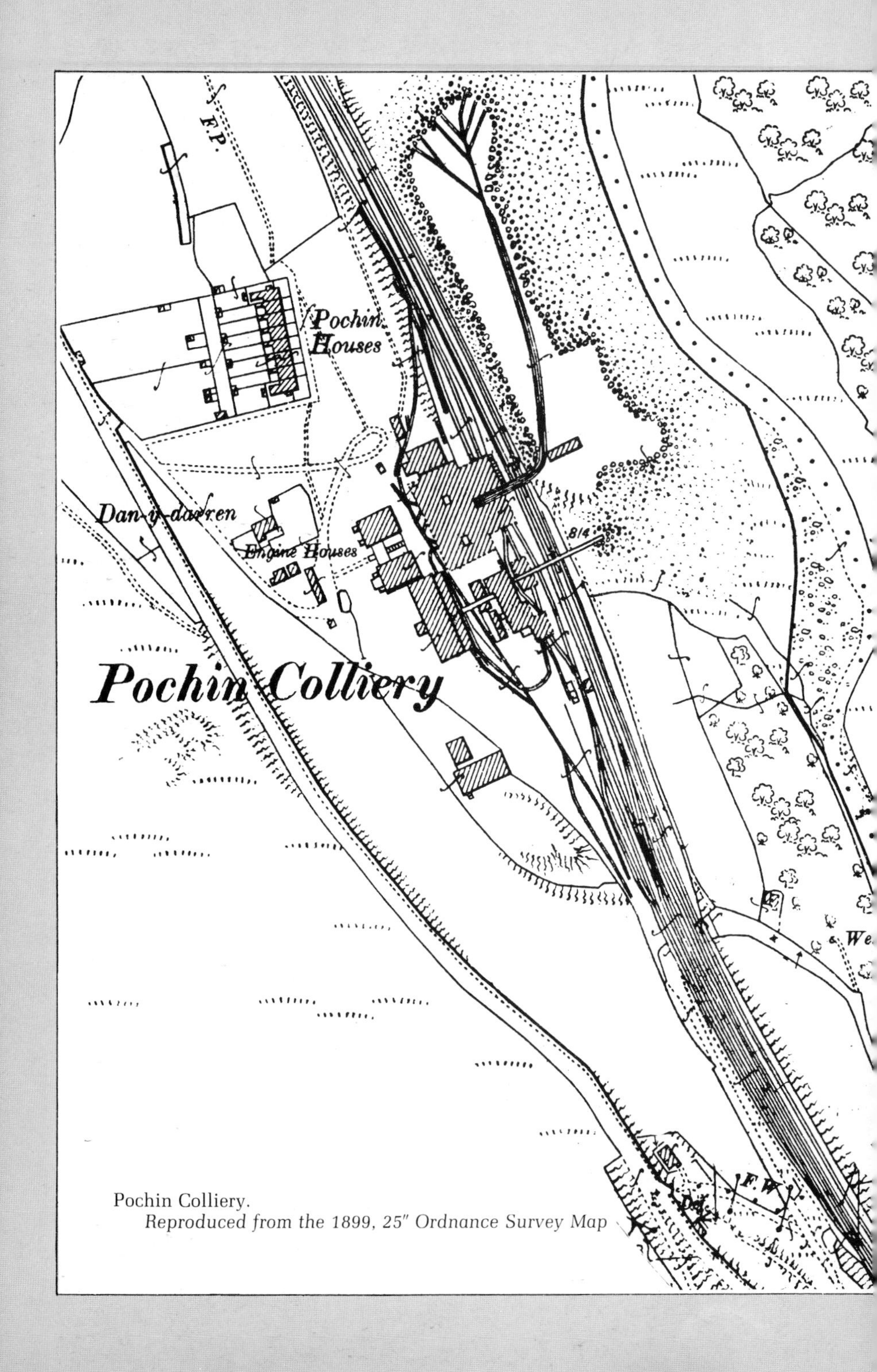

Pochin Colliery.
Reproduced from the 1899, 25″ Ordnance Survey Map

Two views of Pochin Colliery, near Tredegar, both photographed around the turn of the century. The sinking of the shafts at this colliery commenced in 1880 and the details of the two shafts were; No. 1 was 16 ft in diameter and 1347 ft deep with No. 2 shaft being 18 ft in diameter and 1347 ft deep. In the lower view, looking south, the up platform can be seen. *Author's Collection*

Ex LNWR 0–6–2T, No. 58933 seen here leaving Bedwellty Pits Halt with the 1.10 pm from Newport on 19th August, 1950. *Author's Collection*

Bedwellty Pits Halt, seen from the Newport train on the wet day of 13th September, 1951. Note the wooden platform. *H.C. Casserley*

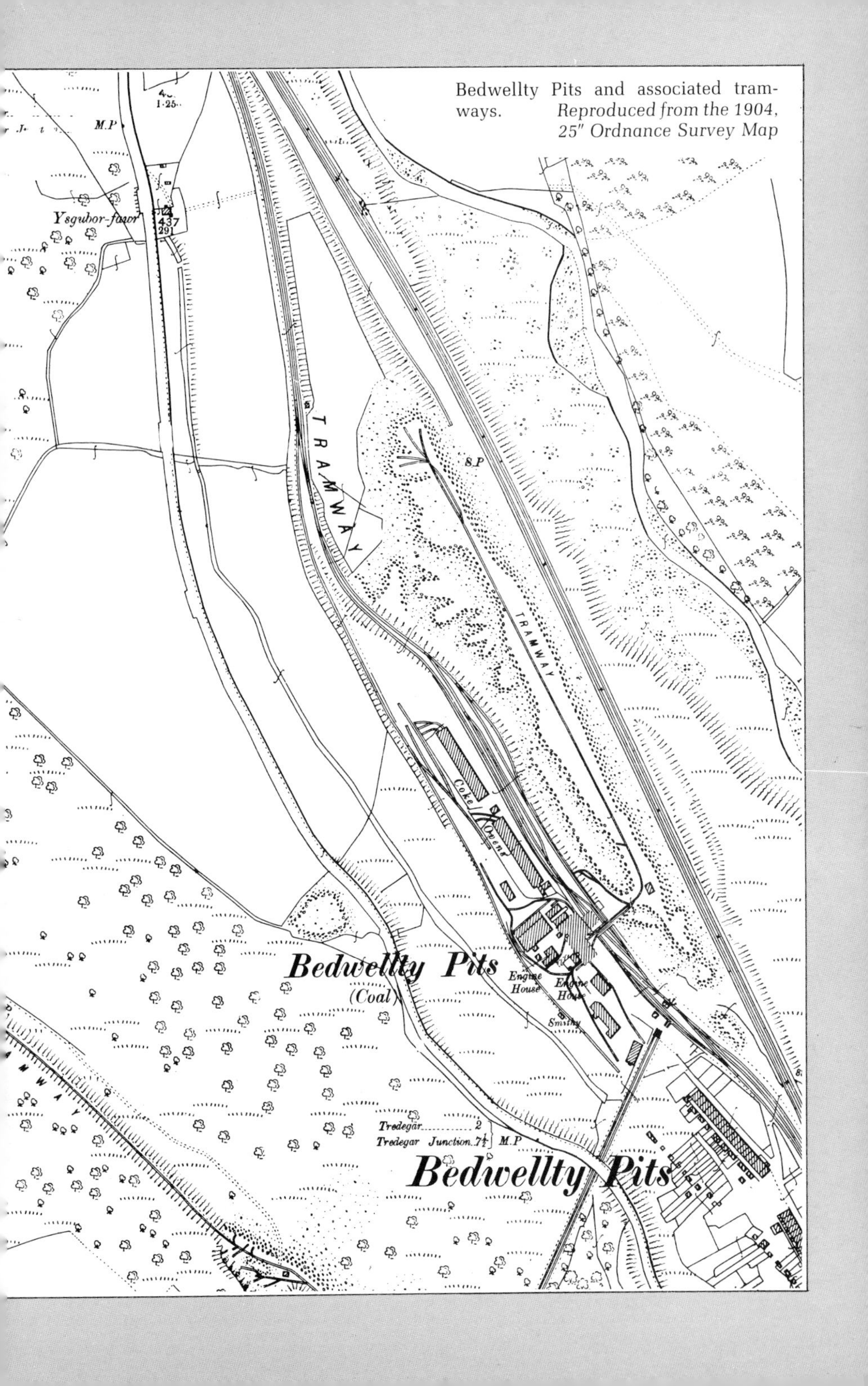

Bedwellty Pits and associated tramways. *Reproduced from the 1904, 25″ Ordnance Survey Map*

Bedwellty Pits Colliery sidings with empties waiting to go under the screens for loading. *Author's Collection*

N.C.B. Peckett, 0–4–0ST *Sir John Wyndham Beynon* on the ex-TIC line at Tredegar with a train of recovered coal from Ty-Trist/Whitworth Colliery tips in April 1966. *R.H. Marrows*

The Mill Farm and Ty-Trist Colliery near Tredegar; derelict buildings abound in the valley, seen here on 6th June, 1956. *Gordon Hayward*

Whitworth Colliery near Tredegar. *Author's Collection*

A fine view of six of the Tredegar Iron and Coal Company's locomotives (and staff) in their yard at Tredegar before 1905. Note some of

An LMS view of the station from the footbridge at Tredegar in the late 1930's. This brick building replaced the LNWR wooden structure in 1932. The bookstall disappeared soon after this photograph was taken. *Author's Collection*

A view of Tredegar station looking towards Nantybwch on 13th September, 1951. *H.C. Casserley*

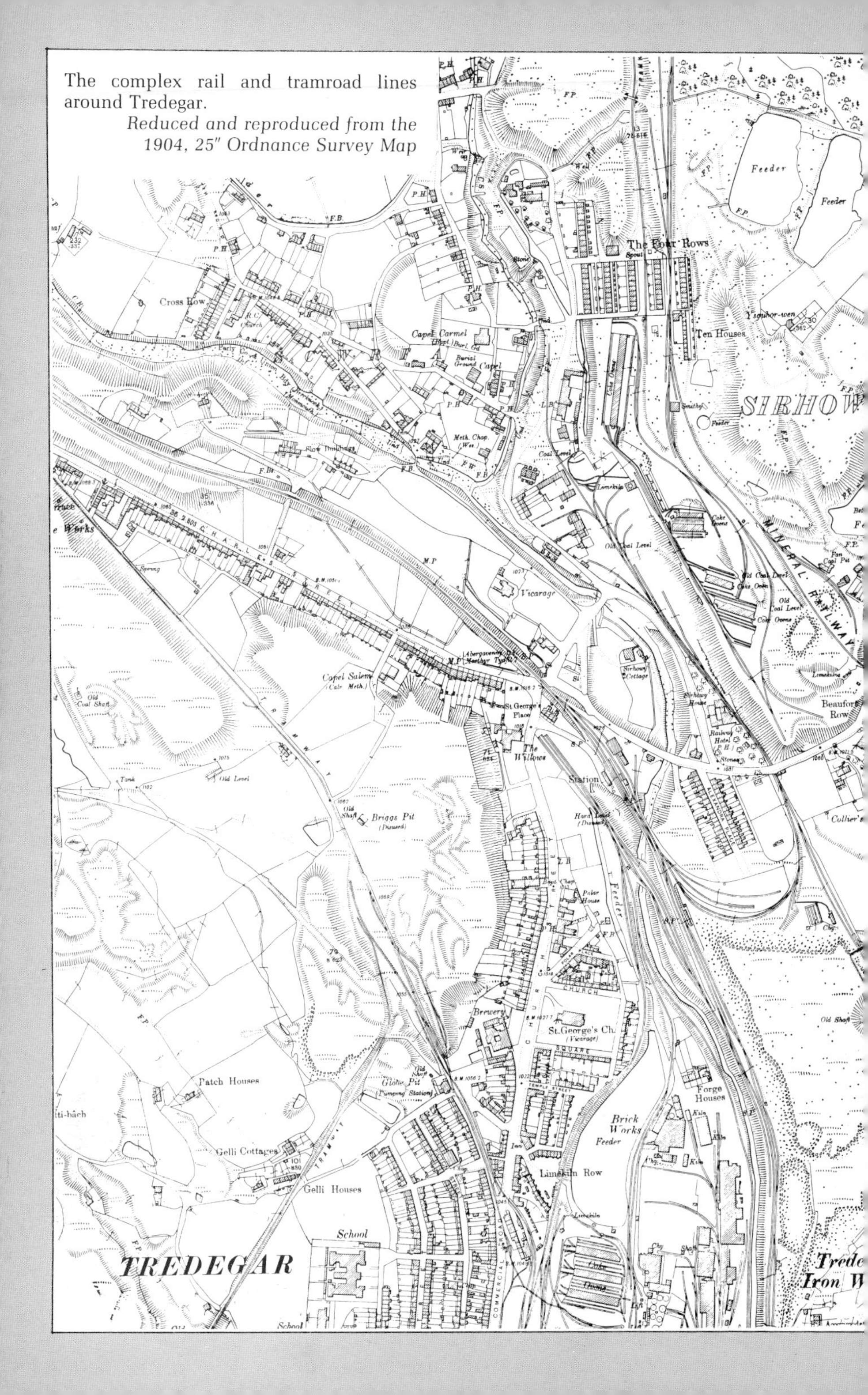

The complex rail and tramroad lines around Tredegar.

Reduced and reproduced from the 1904, 25″ Ordnance Survey Map

Two views of Tredegar station. The top view shows 'Coal' tank No. 7829 on the Newport to Nantybwch train soon after the introduction of the vestibule and corridor stock on 30th September, 1935. Next to the locomotive is ex-LNWR brake third corridor coach, followed by LMS brake-3rd vestibule coach. The lower view shows an ex-GWR 0–6–0PT on an auto train service in the 1950s.

Courtesy Welsh Railways Research Circle and Lens of Sutton

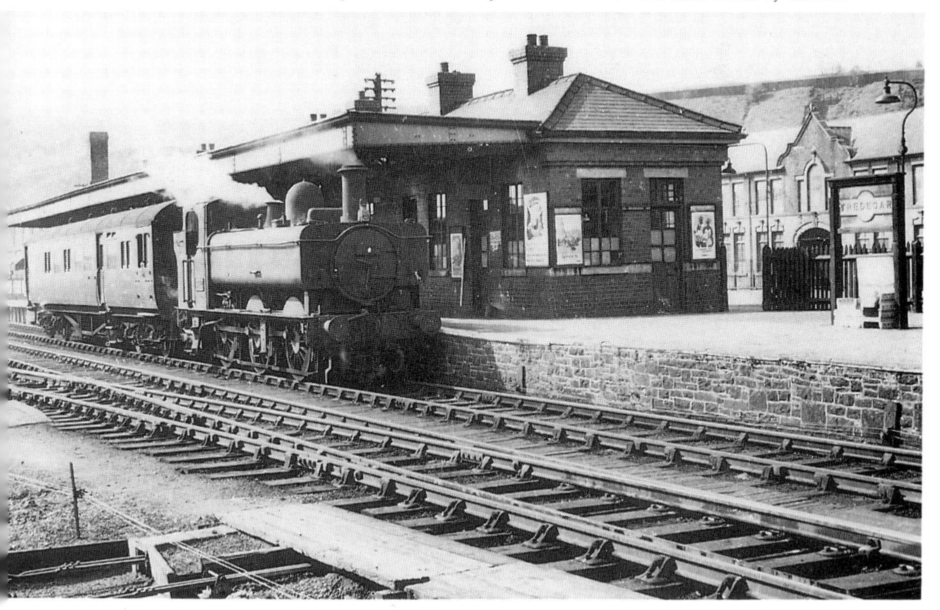

A view of Tredegar level crossing and No. 1 signal box on 13th July, 1958. Note the two-way signal post located in the Tredegar Iron & Coal Co's yard beyond the bridge.
H.C. Casserley

Ex-LNWR 0–8–0s No. 49064 and 49121 seen here at Tredegar shed in 1957 (note the cabbed tenders).
Pendon Museum

Tredegar brick works near Sirhowy station with Private Owner wagons being loaded.
Author's Collection

Navigation Colliery, Sirhowy (owned by Graham Brothers Ltd). Note the two styles of P.O. wagon lettering.
Author's Collection

A good view of Sirhowy station, seen facing Tredegar on 13th July, 1958.
H.C. Casserley

A school trip awaiting the arrival of their service from Nantybwch, post 1956. The covered accommodation at this station was very limited so it was lucky it wasn't raining.
D. Bowen

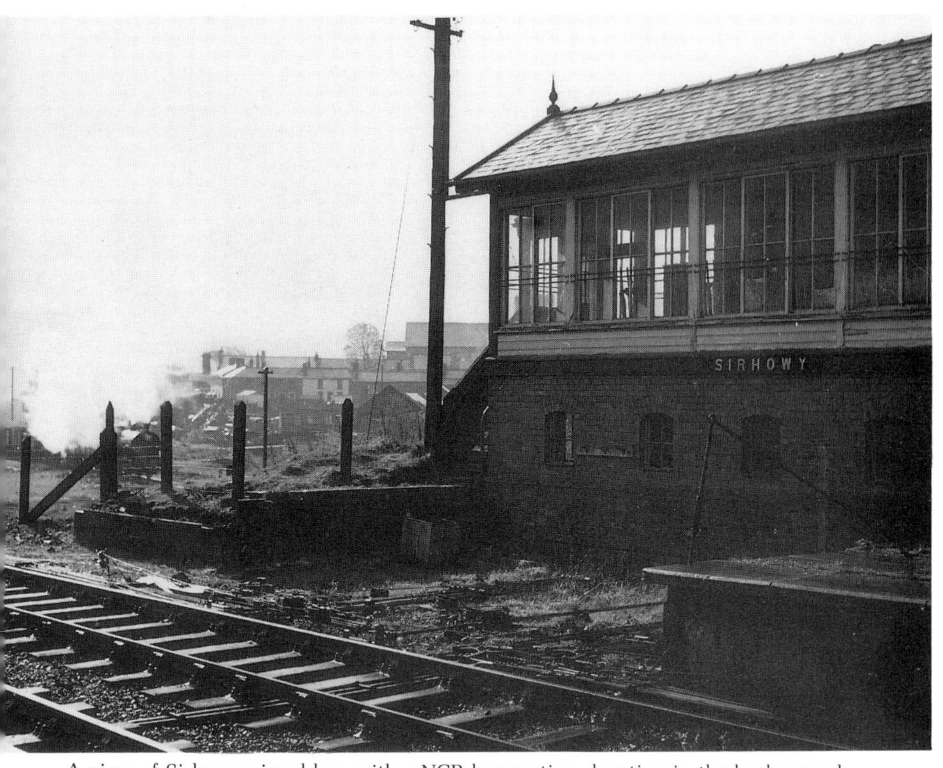

A view of Sirhowy signal box with a NCB locomotive shunting in the background.
Gerald Davies

Sirhowy station looking towards Tredegar in the 1960s, note the wooden platform extension.
Lens of Sutton

Nantybwch Junction station with its tightly curved platform (note the check-rail). The sign by the footbridge reads 'Goods trains to stop, to pin-down brakes'. The Abergavenny–Merthyr platforms are out of sight on the right. Photographed 5th January, 1958. *H.C. Casserley*

A Newport train at Nantybwch station, led by 0–6–2T No. 58915 on 13th September, 1951. *H.C. Casserley*

Chapter Five

Incidents

With a ruling gradient of something like 1 in 100, the Sirhowy Line naturally had its share of runaways; most of these were coal trains, especially in the early part of the century. As turned out, the 'Coal' side tanks did not have much in the way of brake power, and most of the 8-ton wagons were braked on one side only. One December morning in 1916, my father was standing on Argoed down platform waiting for the 8.56 am down passenger, when around the common above the station came a runaway coal train. It passed through with brake whistle sounding, enveloped in coal dust, the van hardly discernible. It was a train of small coal (slack) and fortunately the line was clear; it came to rest in Ynysddu platform, some five miles away. It was the usual practice for the brakesman to pin down sufficient wagon brakes as the train was pulling away from the 'picking-up' point. Experience taught them how many to pin down, and a touch of the whistle from the driver decided this.

Fortunately, fatal accidents were few and far between on the Sirhowy Branch but the *Monmouthshire Merlin* for 31st August, 1877 recorded how a coal train was proceeding up the bank from Tredegar at night when the coupling snapped and eight wagons and the brake van ran wild; the guard jumping clear and escaped with a few scratches. The train demolished three wagons, a 4-wheel coach and the crossing gates at Tredegar. Another report, from the *South Wales Argus* this time, for 18th December, 1902 describes how a coal train, in a similar position on the bank (1 in 37 in places) ran back through Sirhowy station and on to Tredegar at speed, crashing into three engines, a van, and some loaded wagons, the brake van reduced to matchwood. Tredegar station was completely closed to traffic. One company's servant was killed.

On Saturday 26th August, 1933 another accident occurred at Tredegar Junction Lower, when the 9.05 pm ex-Newport, which had been detained at the up home signal, was just starting to move forward when it was struck in the rear by an engine and van, which had been permitted to follow before the up passenger train had cleared the section. The speed of the engine and van was not high, but the passenger train was well loaded, and 53 passengers complained of minor injuries, and one passenger and the guard of the passenger train were detained in hospital. The train consisted of eight 4-wheelers, made up of one 3-coach close-coupled unit, one Third Brake, another 3-coach close-coupled unit, and another Third Brake, in that order. The last vehicle had the guard's compartment at the leading end, and two ordinary compartments at the trailing end. The engine was 'Coal' side tank No. 7831. The following train consisted of 0–8–0 tender engine No. 8934 and one 20-ton goods brake. The only damage to No. 8934 was a fracture of the right-hand buffer plunger and leading buffer plank slightly bent. The leading end of the rear coach rode up on to the trailing end of the coach ahead, which resulted in telescoping of both coaches, and one pair of wheels was derailed.

The signalman at Tredegar Lower Junction said that the up line block instruments were at 'Train on line' at the time and that no bell signals were made offering or accepting the engine and van. When the signalman at Nine Mile Point No. 2 Box telephoned to say he had allowed the engine and brake to proceed, the Lower Junction signalman intended to allow his standing passenger train to proceed forward to his box or starting signal, and then replace his home signal immediately afterwards in order to protect the passenger train and avert a collision, but he was just too late in doing this. It seems responsibility for the accident rested with the signalman at Nine Mile Point No. 2 Box.

The *South Wales Argus* again gave a very detailed report:

> Two persons are in hospital and 27 others were injured and the guards van and one coach were partly telescoped and splinters of wood and smashed glass were strewn over the permanent way. The guard of the train, Harry Roberts, of 16, Ashvale, Tredegar, sustained head injuries and a badly bruised leg and David Evans, a blacksmith at Tredegar Works, of Mydrin Place, Sirhowy, had his leg crushed and suffered severely from shock. These two were conveyed to Tredegar Hospital and detained.
>
> The force of the impact was so great that the guards van was telescoped by the coach immediately in front of it, and the last compartment of the passenger coach was completely demolished. Roberts was found by Mr Blackett*, a clerk at Blackwood station, wedged between pieces of broken timber and he had to obtain the assistance of other railwaymen to extricate him. Dr A.L. Evans, Pontllanfraith and Dr Kendrick, Blackwood, assisted by ambulance men and women, including Mrs Kendrick were quickly on the scene and rendered valuable assistance, as also did Police Sergeant Williams, Blackwood, P.C. Harris, Pontllanfraith, and P.C. W. Prince, Blackwood. Mr Blackett, Clerk at Blackwood station, a passenger in the train, organised matters until the arrival of Mr Bently, Station Master, Pontllanfraith, while Mr Story, Traffic Manager and Inspector Jarman, Abergavenny motored to the scene, with staff from Tredegar Locomotive and Engineering Depts. Railway Officials and Staff members worked hard on the scene of the accident including Mr Michael, Station Master, Blackwood.

For some reason, railway terminology nearly always baffles the public and the press. The term 'Light Engine' means 'Engine only' and not a *light* engine! The remarks of one passenger were 'It was fortunate too that the engine that ran into the train was of the light type and not the heavy or I do not know what would have happened'. In fact, it was an engine and van that ran into the passenger train. Incidentally, the engine concerned, 0–8–0 No. 8934, would be placed in the medium to heavy class! It is worth noting the formation of the train, which was made up of odd sets, and had some bearing on the injuries involved – if the last vehicle, which was a 4-wheel Compo Brake had been the correct way around, the guard would have probably been the only person injured.

Relying again on our local paper *The South Wales Argus*, there is a report of a gas explosion at Pontllanfraith High Level station on Monday 20th October, 1952. The explosion occurred early on the Monday morning when the porter, Mr Mason was going on duty about 4.30 am. The premises had

*Mr Blackett was later appointed Station Master at Four Ashes, near Stafford.

been closed during the weekend, and gas which had been leaking in the booking office, filled the room and blew up on coming into contact with the waiting room light. Mr Mason received cuts from flying glass to both his hands and was attended by Dr Gordon Mackay. Afterwards he was sent home. Mr Bassett, the crossing box signalman, saw the explosion from the window, and said glass and office papers went into the air for a distance of some 40 yards. The booking office was wrecked and the window frames broken. The office clock stopped at 4.31 am but was not damaged. The glass of the platform clock was blown out and the hands could not be found. Station routine was not affected – 'We served workmen with tickets through one of the broken windows' the station master, Mr Summerhill said.

I will conclude by relating a true story illustrating the art of bringing a runaway to a gradual stop without excessive damage. At the time, my father was at Markham Village, a small station on the Sirhowy Branch about five miles below Tredegar, in the early part of 1931. At about 1.30 pm, the signalman at Markham Village box received the 'runaway' emergency bell signal from the signalman at Bedwellty Pits. A telephone message gave the information that a GW 'Macaw' and brake van had just passed his box and was gaining speed. There was already a down 'mineral' in the section between Markham Village and Argoed; in fact it was in the act of picking up loaded wagons from Abernant Colliery – the train and brake standing on the main line, while the engine was inside picking up. The decisive move here was that the engine was quickly brought back on to its train, and the driver asked to pull forward at 12–15 mph, and while doing this, the runaway made contact with the moving train, doing only superficial damage to the headstocks. Meanwhile, the guard took cover in Abernant Colliery sidings. The action averted what could have been a nasty accident. There is little trace now of Abernant Colliery and sidings or Abernant No. 2 box, which was the outlet for the colliery.

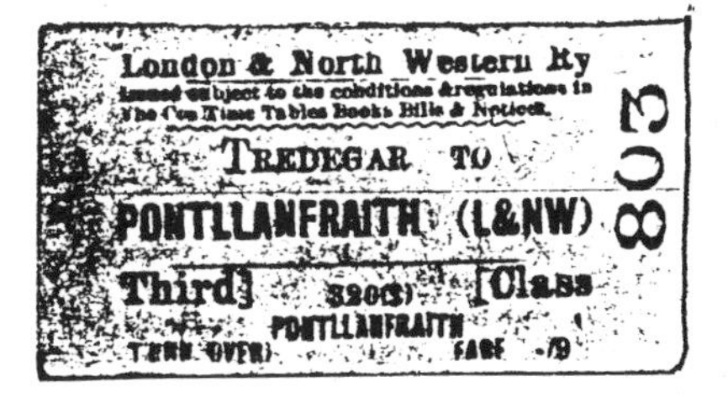

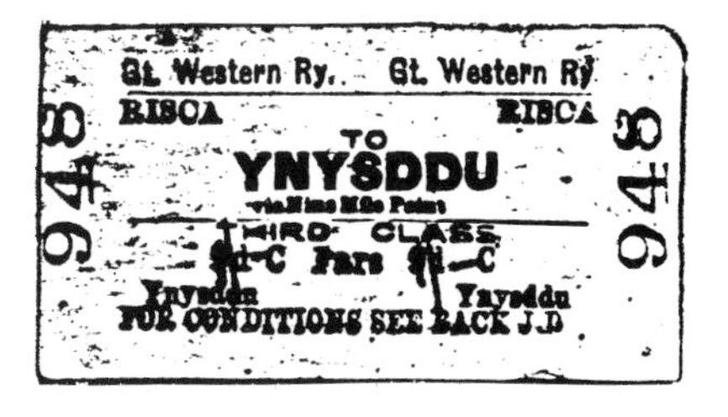

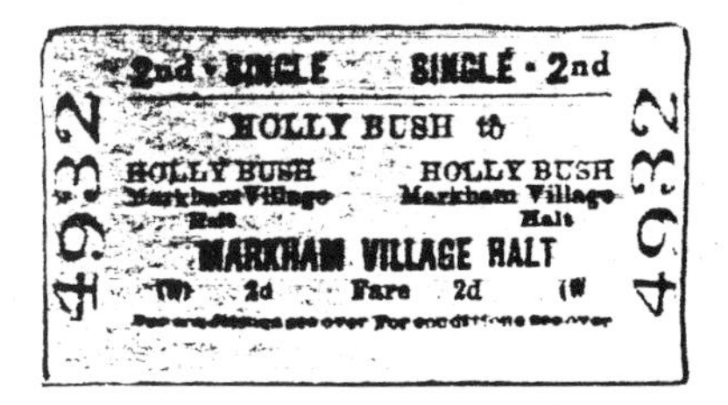

An 0–6–2 'Coal' Tank, No. 7822 and shed staff at Tredegar shed. As LNWR No. 1256 it was at Blaenavon in 1917 and then by 1922, at Tredegar. *Courtesy Graham Jones*

LMS locomotive No. 27663 seen here in 1939 at Tredegar shed. This locomotive was built July 1883 to Crewe No. 2661, as LNWR No. 110. It was renumbered in LMS days to 7663 and scrapped in December 1947. *Author's Collection*

Chapter Six

Officers and Staff and Some Signalling Notes

Officers controlling the district from 'North Western' days include Joseph Bishop, J.A. Findlay (son of Sir George Findlay, General Manager LNWR), A.T. Cotton, E. Goulbourn and C.H. Tait, district superintendents, Abergavenny. H.M. Bradford, C.O. Cotton, A.G.T. Possnett, C.R. Irving, N.L. Wallis and W.H. Power, were District Engineers at different times.

The Engineers had their own inspection coupé (combined coach and tender). The engine was one of Allen's 6 ft small firebox 2–2–2s No. 135 *Bat*, built at Crewe in 1852. As *Locomotion* No. 3082 she became *Engineer South Wales* in 1911 and was scrapped in 1920. This engine was followed by one of the LNW 2–4–0 'Jumbo's' No. 485 *Euxine* which remained until 1933, after which the job was passed on to a Midland 2–4–0 No. 155 transferred from Bristol, afterwards renumbered 20155. The latter left Abergavenny in 1946, and was the last of the special engines allocated to the District Engineer's Dept. When the Midland 2–4–0 took over she was attached to a former L&YR 6-wheel Saloon.

Mr F.J. Mansfield, the deputy at the district traffic superintendent's office at Abergavenny commenced his railway career with the LNWR at Swansea in 1881. He served under five superintendents in all at Abergavenny and was an authority on the Railway Clearing House Rule Book, and usually passed station masters and signalmen on the Company's Rules and Regulations. The 'North Western' Directors' specials covered most of the system from time to time and made several visits into the Sirhowy Valley. When they did come, it was Phil Lloyd, proprietor of the Argoed Arms Hotel who catered for them. While they were at lunch, the engine and coach would stand in Rhoswen sidings. Engines and stock varied from the 0–6–2 'Coal Tank', LNW 2–4–0 tender engines, and occasionally the engine *Cornwall* and a 12-wheel Dining Car.

The Control Office was transferred to Abergavenny, Brecon Road, in 1929; before this it was situated on the down Merthyr platform at Nantybwch. The controller was W.B. Shelton, with a staff of three on each eight hour shift. Mr Shelton later became assistant superintendent at Abergavenny.

Little is known of the staff relating to the Sirhowy Railway except of the key positions appointed at the time. The General Manager was S.H. Yockney, traffic manager, Robert Bond, and locomotive superintendent, Benjamin Samuel Fisher. Mr Bond had been station master at Newport (High Street) prior to his appointment at Tredegar. Many of the station masters taken over by the LNW in 1876 had seen service on the Sirhowy Railway – Robert O'Connor, Nantybwch; Harry Duck, Sirhowy; John Hutchings, Tredegar; Robert Howell, Argoed; Cornelius Bohane, Blackwood; David Owen, Pontllanfraith; Stephen Morgan and William Morgan, Ynysddu; and William Francis and A.T. Robinson, Nine Mile Point. John Saunders, a Sirhowy Railway passenger guard worked until the early 1890s. Incidentally Cornelius Bohane, of Blackwood was also a poet and would often express his views in verse when a local celebrity passed through Blackwood station.

Locomotive and crew outside Markham Village signal box after picking-up colliers' coaches at Nantybwch in 1957. The locomotive was 0–8–0 No. 49409. *Left to right:* Guard: Lyn Williams, Driver: G. Rowlands and Fireman: John Taylor.

Author's Collection

My father at Markham Village, 1928, A.T. Tasker (station master) with porter and linesman.

Author's Collection

There were many gatherings of railway staff in the early days – *The Monmouthshire Merlin* mentions a Supper at the George Inn, Mount Street, Tredegar on 11th January, 1878 given to the Sirhowy Line section of the LNWR. Officials attending were G. Bamford, T. Robinson, J. Kevenagh, A. Hunt, John Hutchings (station master), J.E. Lewis, George Hutchings, R. Jarman, W. Davies and R. Davies, Sirhowy Branch inspector. A Mr Pickwick was clerk-in-charge at Tredegar in 1900.

During World War I a 'War Seal Foundation Fund' was set up and meetings were held throughout the war period at various places, collecting quite large sums of money for the railway staff involved in the War effort. Members for the Tredegar area included A. Price (station master), E.J. Watkins, C. Singer (Treasurer), Fred O'Connor, Charles Carter (station master), T. Jenks, W. Williams, Charles Meale, J.B. Turner, R. Carter, Miss Thomas and station clerks Hill, Millward and Watkins. A similar set-up was organised at Hollybush by J.F. Davies, station master, T.C. Lewis, station master, Markham Village, and John Thomas, signalman, Hollybush. Local Collieries also helped – there was a good relationship between them and the railways – both customers!

Mr Singer, mentioned above, was involved in a fatal accident at Tredegar in January 1926; he was attaching two colliers' coaches behind the 8.45 pm passenger train which had just arrived from Newport when he slipped and fell, the coach wheels passing over his legs. Many will remember inspector Jarman, who retired in 1934, and inspector Richards who was well liked by the staff at Tredegar.

Among the more prominent members of the staff who served the public well over the years was Mr Price, station master, Tredegar who retired in 1923. He commenced his railway career in the LNW Goods Dept, Ebbw Vale in 1877 and became station master at Gilwern in 1887, Beaufort in 1893, and prior to coming to Tredegar was district signalman's & staff inspector at Abergavenny. Mr G.H. Davies followed Mr Price at Tredegar. Another very popular station master on the Sirhowy Branch was Mr Henry Forrester of Blackwood – Blackwood was rather different then; much of the town's business centred near the station at that time. The platforms were a mass of colour in the spring and summer. For some years the station master lived in the house situated at the north end of the down platform. Mr Forrester had held the position of station master at Sirhowy, Dowlais and Ebbw Vale before retiring from Blackwood. His son, Chris Forrester, was senior clerk at Blackwood for many years, and before his retirement, was station master in the Bournemouth area.

Our resumé of station masters would not be complete without mention of Mr George Morgan, who was station master at Pont Lawrence until his retirement in 1928. Born in Argoed in 1862, Mr Morgan started work there in 1879. He was later promoted signalman, and was the first to work at Nine Mile Point No. 2 Box, which was opened in 1894, and where bees hived in the ventilators. He was a wonderful character, with a warm welcoming smile for all passing through Pont Lawrence.

T.W. Slade, who was signalman at Pontllanfraith Crossing Box until 1937,

Sirhowy signal box. This was the old box at the Tredegar end of the down platform. The new box was situated on the up platform. *Gerald Davies*

A very early photograph of the staff at Tredegar station. The man in the bowler hat is presumed to be Mr Pickwick (clerk-in-charge) and next on the left is Mr John Hutchings (station master). *Courtesy the late Oliva Ashton*

A group photograph of 29th January, 1923 of Tredegar station staff. The fourth from the left (*front row*) was Inspector Richards. *Author's Collection*

was responsible for diverting two runaway coaches from the main line at Pontllanfraith in 1931. The coaches had come from Tredegar, and Mr Slade, having received the 'runaway' signal on the block bells, turned the coaches from the main line on to the machine road where they came into contact with a goods brakevan doing considerable damage. Ernest Rees and Walter Hill were very well known in the lower part of the Valley; the former as station master Ynysddu, promoted to Abergavenny (Brecon Road) in 1932, later covering the Junction as well when Sam Beard retired. Walter Hill was booking clerk at Blackwood then station master, Pontllanfraith, retiring as chief clerk Penrith.

During World War I thousands of women clerks were employed – Sirhowy Goods was entirely staffed by women, five in all! Many other stations on the branch had women booking clerks – Tredegar, Hollybush, Argoed, Blackwood and Pontllanfraith. In sharp contrast to today, all except one was single!

Coming now to the passenger guards and drivers; my father could just remember guard Saunders a few years before his retirement. In those days, the train was the only service to Newport and business people who required small items urgently relied entirely on John Saunders for this unofficial service which worked extremely well. Travelling with him in the van my father occasionally heard the rather pertinent remark 'Not much over'. This referred to the amount of change after the purchase, which, by agreement was usually his!

The guards of pre-grouping days included Elijah Edworthy, Teddy Powell, and J.B. Turner, who retired in 1928. The latter had what must be a unique experience for a passenger guard. He once picked up a dog at Risca station, destined for Pontllanfraith. The dog was duly leashed to a ring on the van side provided for this purpose, and all seemed in order. However, the lead proved to be too long and although Guard Turner got into his van alright at Risca, he failed to make an entry at Nine Mile Point, Pont Lawrence or Ynysddu, having made this part of the journey on the van footboard! Other passenger guards who served in LMS days were Haines, Michael, Watkins, Roberts, and Bloomfield.

Driver J. Morgan could well be regarded as 'Father of the shed' at Tredegar, having worked there as a driver for 35 years. Mr Morgan joined the service of the old 'North Western' as a cleaner at Abergavenny in 1873. He retired at 70 years of age in 1923. Tender engine 0–8–0 No. 631 was probably the first of its class at Tredegar – it was shared at that time by Arthur Jones and Jack Roberts through the 24 hours. One of the first 0–6–2 'Coal' side tanks came to Tredegar in 1890 when driver Baker transferred from Abergavenny to Tredegar and brought his engine with him. The running shed foreman, William Baxter, a native of Bridgnorth, Shropshire retired in May 1925, after 51 years service. D.W. Morris, who came from Denbigh was the next shed foreman.

The duties of the district reliefman on the branch in 'North Western' days were not easy; the district inspector's office gave orders by memorandum or telegraph, giving the place and time and you were expected to get there by any means available, much of it on foot. The telegraph needle was still in use in 1906 and my father often received instructions for duty in this way. A good operator on the needle could converse almost at the speed of normal speech. There was no road transport. Instructions for covering station masters on annual and sick leave came from the district office at Abergavenny.

The starting time when covering signalmen could be extremely awkward; they were ten hour shifts (except Tredegar Level Crossing Box, which was eight hours) and duties like 2.00 pm to midnight or 4.00 am to 2.00 pm were not in favour when 12 or 15 miles from home. Passenger trains did not often fit in for reaching work, and advantage was taken of mineral and goods trains, for which passes were issued for riding with the guard. In those days, one could see the last means of transport home disappear in the distance, and the booking-off time would always be after the last passenger train had cleared. Later, boxes could be switched out with trains in the section, giving an opportunity for a ride home.

My father was one of the district relief men for the Merthyr, Tredegar and Abergavenny District and covered all signal boxes and grade 4 and 5 stations. Occasionally, grade 3 stations were covered if staffing problems were acute. Agents at Brynmawr, Sirhowy, Tredegar and Blackwood were usually covered by the chief clerk of the station concerned. Although the main part of the duty consisted of covering annual and sick leave, lever movements had to be taken from time to time, which could effect the grade of the box. It also included the special opening of boxes for the Signal and Telegraph Dept and the Board of Trade. There was plenty of variety – within a period of three months the station masters at Rhymney Bridge, Trevil, Ynysddu and Bedwellty Pits were covered, as well as signalmen at Argoed, Pontllanfraith Level Crossing, and Nine Mile Point No. 2 boxes.

An entry for Friday 10th May, 1907 reads – 'Pilotman between Brynmawr and Nantyglo-travelling with Crane'. My father's diary for 18th December, 1915 (Monday morning) gives some idea of local working and climatic conditions sometimes prevailing: Nantybwch 4.00 am to 2.00 pm, vice signalman Atkinson, sick. Below was a description of the weather; 'gale blowing and snowing'. It meant a walk of eight miles, with occasionally a ride from Tredegar up with engine and brake or empty stock. The first thing to do on arrival was to dry his clothes on the box stove – that is, after lighting it! On the same morning a crow came through the box window, breaking the glass, and careering around, putting the box oil lamp out.

The weather at 1,300 ft can be vicious at times. The late J.M. Dunn summed it up in no uncertain manner when describing the weather in 1922.

> When I drew my curtains about 4.30 am on the 31st of March, 1922, a few flakes of snow had begun to fall, and when I went out at 5.15 am the next morning, I found an engine snowed up between the Sirhowy line platforms at Nantybwch station.

He had the following to say for the year 1927:

> On the 26th of December, 1927 a train with two engines at each end was fast in the snow on the up line at Trevil. The next day five engines were stuck in the snow in a cutting a mile west of Nantybwch; six others between there and Dowlais Top and

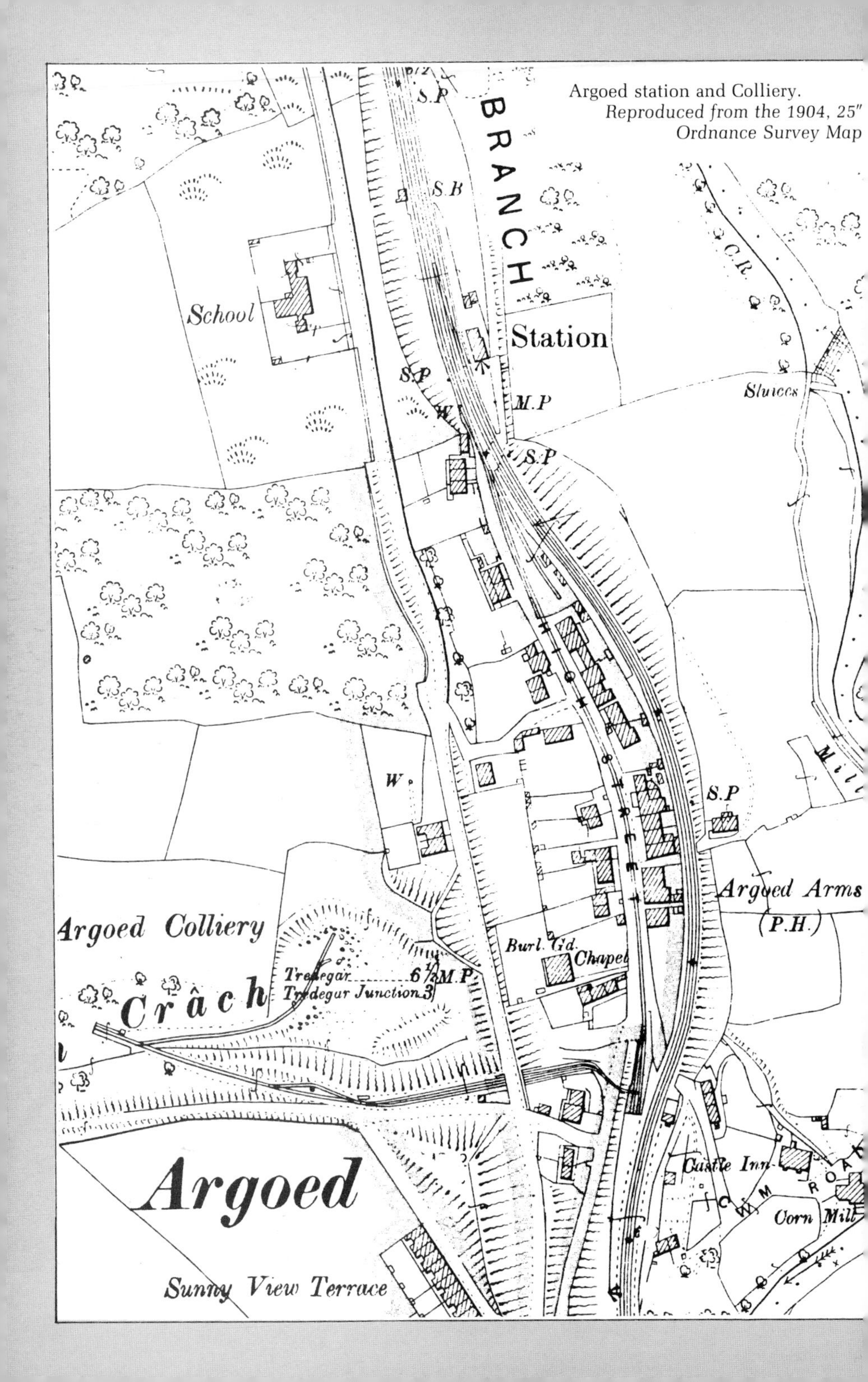

Argoed station and Colliery.
Reproduced from the 1904, 25″ Ordnance Survey Map

Argoed signal box showing the unusual construction. *Author's Collection*

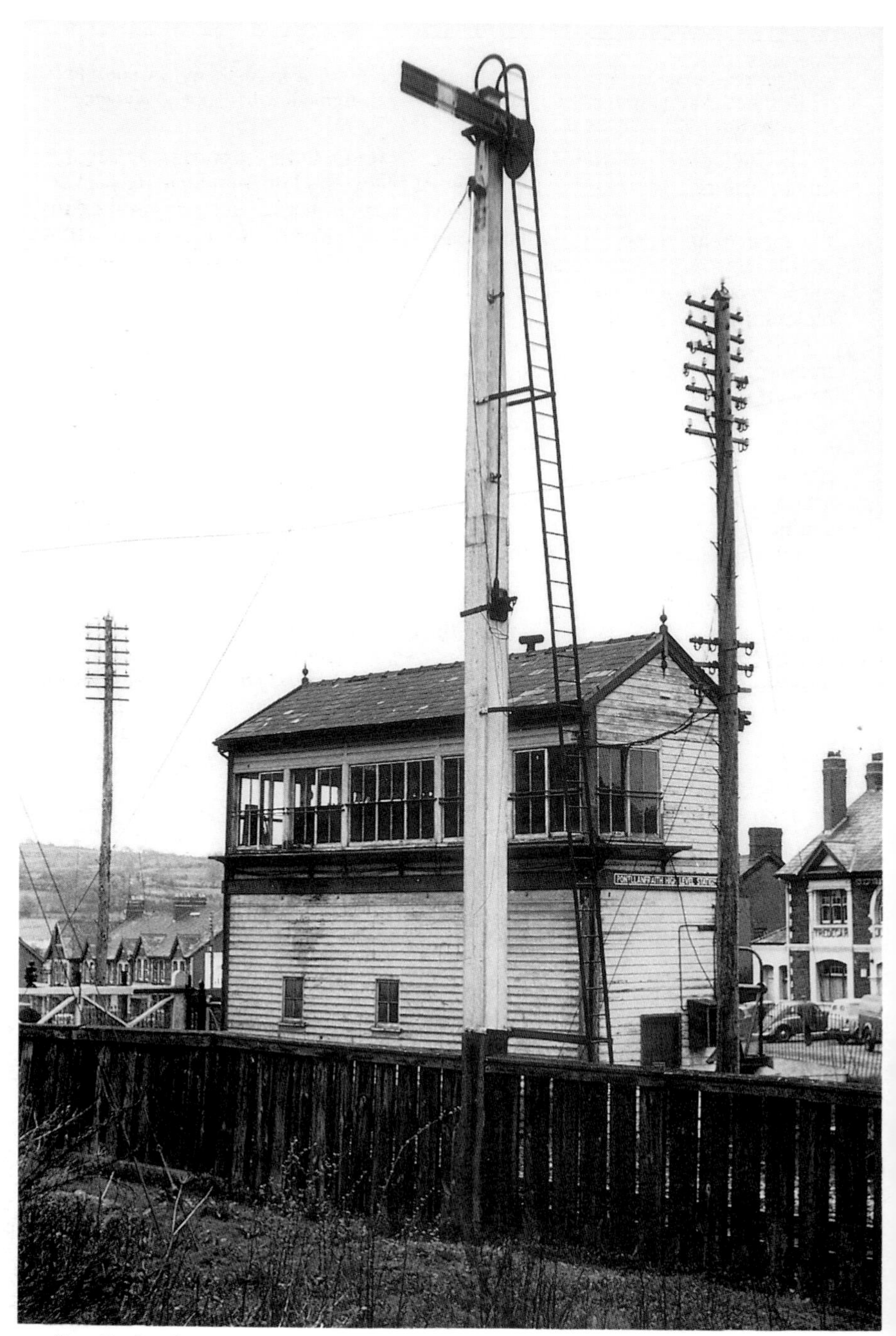

Pontllanfraith station crossing signal box and up home signal. Note the Junction Hotel on the right.
R.H. Marrows

three on the Blaenavon line. The 2.30 pm from Merthyr to Abergavenny got into a drift near Nantybwch an hour later, and there it stopped, with about 40 passengers on board, until 2.30 the next morning.

The Reliefman's duties would not be complete without putting on record one hilarious incident which occurred at Blackwood during the early part of January 1918, when cattle, which had just been unloaded got away and on to the main road, with Mr Forrester, the station master, two clerks from the goods shed, and my father, who was in place of Chris Forrester, the booking clerk, giving chase down the main road towards the town. However, by 11 o'clock in the morning they were all back in their pen!

In 1920 my father was offered the vacancy of station master & goods agent in Abersychan & Talywain, but the fact was we were very deeply rooted at Argoed, in the Sirhowy Valley, with our own house and many friends – it was the last straw; particularly for my mother, who refused to move into a company's house! Fortunately, my father knew, by that time, some of the people who mattered at Abergavenny, and with a little delicate persuasion, asked if he could take the vacancy at Markham Village, which was also available at the same time; this they eventually agreed upon, my father remaining there until his retirement in November 1933.

Notes on Signal Boxes

Tredegar Level Crossing and South End boxes (Tredegar No. 1 & No. 2) had the most lever movements over the years in the 24 hours. As much of the shunting was made over the crossing, an eight-hour shift could mean moving the gates 50 to 60 times. Every up train coming to a stand at the platform must have the gates in its favour, even if it was not going forward. The

Ty-Trist siding signal box; looking north, this was a new box opened 24th February, 1936, where the signalman worked with his back to the track – the only one like it on the branch. *Courtesy Gerald Davies*

signalman had to meet every train in each direction with the staff. The box had a double column staff machine, coloured red and blue, but in 1937 these were replaced by electric key tokens. The crossing box had a 50 lever frame, with 44 in use in 1938, open 24 hours. Tredegar No. 2 (South End) controlled engines on and off the shed. It had a 40 lever frame, with 34 in use in 1938, open 24 hours. The sections between Tredegar South End and Nantybwch were single track. There was a crossing loop at Sirhowy.

Nantybwch and Sirhowy boxes were situated on the platform. Sirhowy station had three boxes in its time; in one instance (from 1891 to c.1927) the track went under the box. Pontllanfraith Crossing Box had a 50 lever frame, with 45 in use in 1938. It was open 24 hours, and access to the box was by inside steps. Abernant No. 1 (Markham Village) had a 35 lever frame, with 27 in use in 1938, and was open 17¾ hours. The Tredegar Iron & Coal Co's private siding here had the Ames electric locking controlled from the box. There was a 20 lever frame at Argoed with all 20 in use; it was open 14½ hours in 1938. Handbells were used at these boxes to warn of the approach of passenger trains until approximately 1924.

Signal Boxes and Cross-Over Roads

Nantybwch No. 1 (2)
Sirhowy
Tredegar (Level Crossing)
Tredegar (South End)
Ty Trist (1)
Bedwellty Pits (2)
Pochin (2)
Hollybush (2)
Abernant No. 1 (2) (Markham Village)
Abernant No. 2 (1)
Rhoswen Sidings (1)
Argoed (1)
Blackwood No. 1 (1)
Blackwood No. 2 (2)
Pontllanfraith (1)
Tredegar Jn Lower (1)
Wyllie No. 1 (1)
Wyllie No. 2 (1)
Ynysddu (1)
Nine Mile Point No. 1 (1)
Nine Mile Point No. 2 (1)

Numbers in brackets indicate number of crossovers.

The 10.38am Newport to Nantybwch train leaving Markham Village on 25th November, 1936 with Stanier 2–6–2T No. 79 in charge. *Author's Collection*

Chapter Seven

Locomotive Miscellany

The class of engine first used by the LNW on the branch seems to have escaped record. Certainly the 0–6–0 saddle tanks (Crewe special shunters) appeared very early, but when they replaced the Sirhowy Railway saddle tank engines is difficult to say. By 1890 there were some LNW 0–6–0 tender 'coal' engines in use. Locomotive water supplies were not good at the time, so perhaps preference was given to the tender engine to carry water.

According to the late J.M. Dunn, the following engines were shedded at Tredegar on 1st January, 1922:

1 0–6–0 saddle tank (Cabless)
2 0–8–0 tender engines – Nos. 631 and 1329. (Both cabbed tender.)
23 0–6–2 side tank 'Coal' engines numbered as follows: 693, 970, 1005, 1053, 1077, 1198, 1203, 1240, 1250, 1254, 1256, 2010, 2351, 2358, 2462, 3325, 3387, 3418, 3702, 3732, 3773, 3774 (all LNW numbers).
Note: 'Coal' Tank LNW No. 1005, later LMS 7705, was withdrawn in November 1946. She had been at Tredegar since 1916.

The following 0–6–2 side tank 'Coal' engines were seen running on the branch between 1930 and 1950:

7690, 7692, 7699, 7705, 7709, 7712, 7717, 7720, 7721, 7730, 7733, 7746, 7768, 7772, 7782, 7814, 7816, 7821, 7822, 7823, 7829, 7831, 7833, 7834, 7835, 7840, 27555, 27585, 27597, 27618, 27631, 27636, 27638, 27657, 27663, 58912. (All LMS & BR Nos.)

At the grouping in 1923, all but eight of the engines survived to receive the LMS numbers 7550–7841, and on the renumbering scheme in 1934, they were allocated the numbers 27550–27681. The 64 that became BR property in 1948, with a few exceptions, were renumbered between 58880 and 58937. The engines were the 'Side Tank' version of the 0–6–0 'Coal Engines'. Three hundred were built between 1881 and 1897.

Some of these had Abergavenny shed allocation numbers: 0–6–2T LNW No. 3353 on shed in 1922, was still working as LMS No. 7746 in 1948; and LNW No. 2358 was still running in 1946 as LMS No. 7840.

Seen between 1930 and 1958 were the following 0–8–0 Tender Engines:

8899, 8921, 8932, 8934, 9064, 9141, 9144, 9161, 9164, 9276, 9402, 49316 and 49409. No. 9064, first seen in 1946, was still at Tredegar in 1958, renumbered 49064. (She was the last LNW engine to leave Tredegar for Ebbw Jn on 8th August, 1959.)

Similarly, there were the following 0–8–4 Side Tank Engines:

7930, 7931, 7932, 7933, 7934, 7935, 7936, 7938, 7939, 7940, 7944, 7945, 7952 and 7956. No. 7930 was numbered LNW 380 when first seen in June 1923, and painted LMS Red.

Other classes based locally were:

Ex-MR 0–6–0 tender engines: 3656, 4347, 4506, 4514.
Ex-MR 0–6–0 tank engines: 7430, 7487.

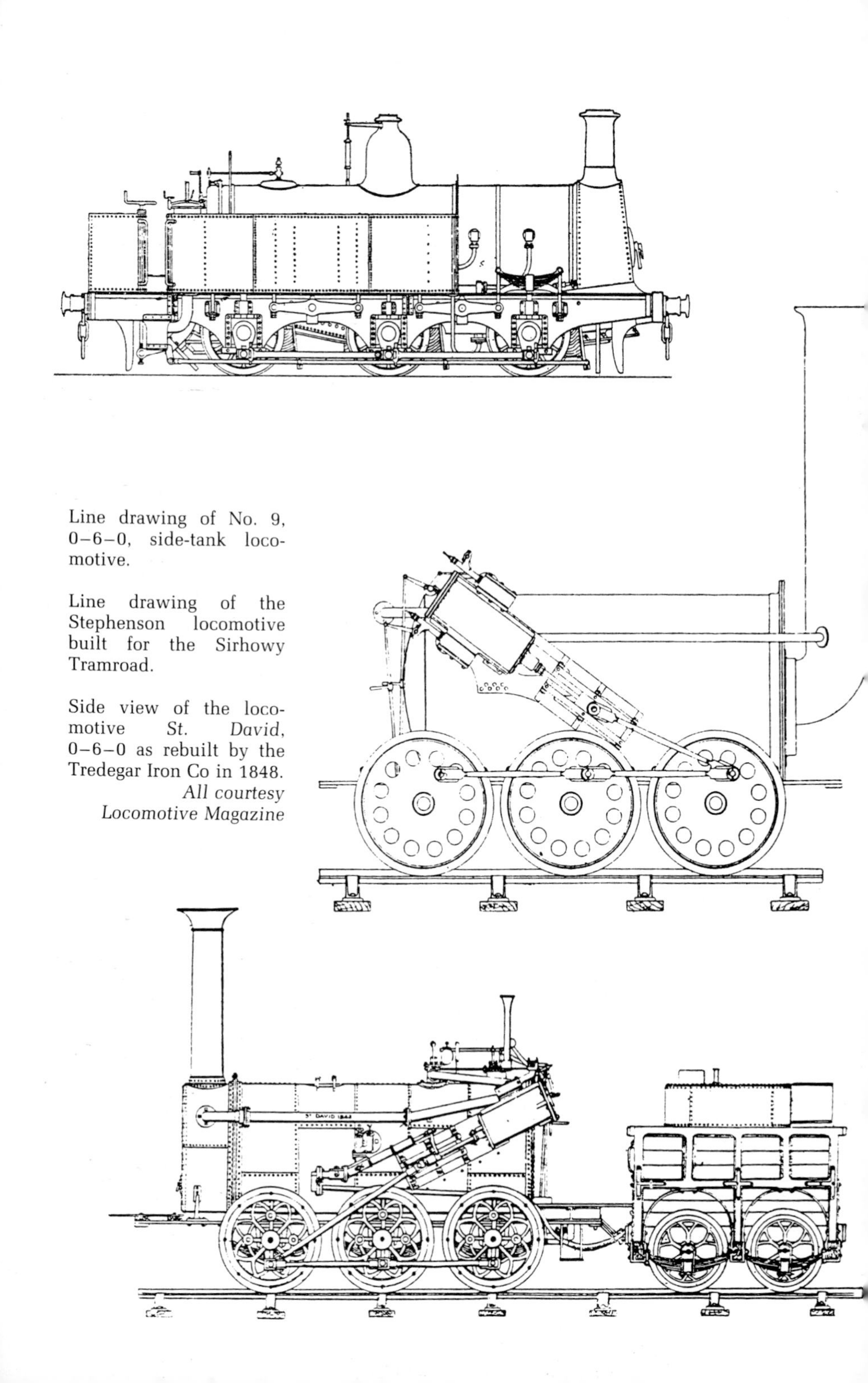

Line drawing of No. 9, 0–6–0, side-tank locomotive.

Line drawing of the Stephenson locomotive built for the Sirhowy Tramroad.

Side view of the locomotive *St. David*, 0–6–0 as rebuilt by the Tredegar Iron Co in 1848.

All courtesy Locomotive Magazine

A fine view of *Bedwellty*, 0–6–0 locomotive on the Sirhowy Tramroad.
Author's Collection

Sirhowy locomotive No. 8, an 0–6–0ST, as built for the Sirhowy Railway Company and used on the line from 1860 to 1876. *Courtesy Locomotive Magazine*

Stanier 2–6–2 Tank Engine No. 79 first appeared on a trial run for platform clearance on 30th March, 1936, and remained on the branch for several years. Her shed number at that time was 7A (Llandudno Junction). Ivatt 2–6–2 Tank Engine No. 1206 was the next to arrive, to be followed by several of the same class. Other locomotives appeared from time to time including the 2–2–2 *Cornwall* (on Directors' specials). LNWR 2–4–0 'Jumbo' class No. 485 and ex-MR 2–4–0 No. 155 (renumbered 20155) were used on District Engineer's duties. LMS 2–6–0 tender engine No. 2930 ('Crab') which was used on excursion traffic, came from Abergavenny shed.

In 1955 there were about a dozen engines at Tredegar shed, consisting of ex-LNW 0–8–0 tender engines and Ivatt 2–6–2 tank engines. By 1958, ex-GW locomotives (0–6–2s and Panniers) had taken over, and Barry Island Sunday Excursion traffic was worked by ex-GW 0–6–2 side tanks from Canton, Cardiff and Ebbw Junction sheds, Newport. From June 1954, passenger trains were worked by the 64XX class auto-fitted Panniers from Ebbw Junction sheds.

The shed at Tredegar had four roads 165 ft long, but a fire in March 1910 destroyed a part of the roof at the inner end, thus restricting its use. It was coded 4E in LMS days. The Breakdown Van at Tredegar in the 1920s was an ex-GC (MSJ&A) 6-wheel Brake Third, converted for suitable accommodation; this was followed by an LNW 6-wheeled passenger van. Locomotive water supplies at Nantybwch were obtained from a brick-lined reservoir. Other water columns were situated at Sirhowy (up platform), Tredegar, Hollybush, Argoed, and Nine Mile Point. Drivers of Sirhowy Valley trains picking up water at Risca on the upward journey placed a card in the box provided at the column.

The sound effects were remarkable, especially on a clear frosty night; that is, sounds peculiar to LNW locomotives. The 'Coal' side tanks produced a chirruping sound when closing the regulator and coasting into the stations on the upward journey. Many of the 0–8–0's leaked at the stuffing box and when working hard would make a wheezy asthmatical sound – no other engine could match them in this respect! As a rule, all down trains had the engine bunker or tender first, the exception being the Barry Excursions, where the engine could be turned ready for the return journey. Many times after the War, one saw one-coach passenger trains hauled by either an 0–8–0 tender engine or 0–8–4 tank, which did not seem quite right somehow.

The 0–8–0's were very prone to slipping, and given the right conditions (drizzle falling) would often come to a stand on the upward journey and remain on the same spot for anything up to ten minutes – the wheels revolving, but making no headway! After an agreed signal had been passed from driver to guard, the van handbrake would be applied and the train would set back on to the van, with all the buffers compressed, and then a mighty tug forward, which sometimes did the trick! It was a precarious business after dark, and it had been known for a train to set back on to the 'catch points' with consequent derailment. On occasions, when time had been lost, the train would be set back on to the down line to allow an up

LNWR 'Coal' tank No. 574 seen here at the back of Heathfields, Tredegar with driver; Mr Herbert Poole on the footplate. These locomotives were the mainstay of local services on the railway. *Author's Collection*

The huge proportions of 0–8–4T No. 380 (in LMS maroon livery), can clearly be seen in this view at Tredegar. This locomotive was first of its class. *Author's Collection*

passenger or colliers' train to pass. Stanier 2–6–2 No. 79 was allocated almost entirely to passenger and colliers' train duties – only once did I see her on a mineral train, one of 39 'empties' and brake, having made it as far as the approach to Argoed station (gradient 1 in 92 rising) and then stalling. Before this, desperate attempts to keep her moving had been made by the fireman throwing ashes on to the rail in front of her, but with little effect. Eventually, a fresh start was made on the reverse curves in the vicinity of Argoed, and she got away without further excessive slipping.

During the last two years before closure the following former Great Western engines were observed:

> 0–6–2T Nos. 5675, 6600 and 6622. These were used on the Sunday Excursions to Barry Island and came from Radyr or Ebbw Junction Sheds.
> 0–6–0T (Panniers) Nos. 3634, 3700, 3712, 6412, 6426, 6427, 6430, 6431, 7721, 7787, 8711, 9644 and 9662. Most of these were used on the Motor Trains.

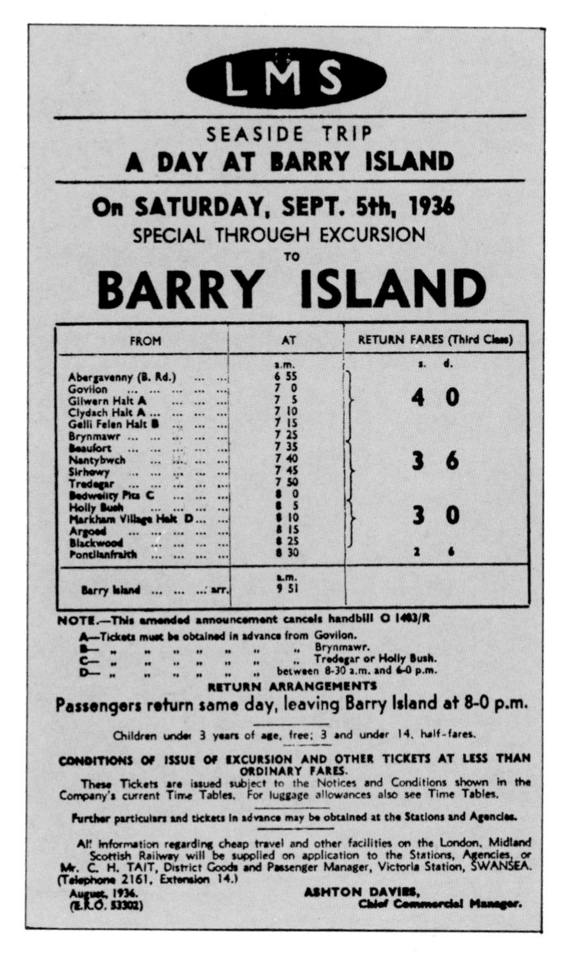

LMS

SEASIDE TRIP

A DAY AT BARRY ISLAND

On SATURDAY, SEPT. 5th, 1936

SPECIAL THROUGH EXCURSION

TO

BARRY ISLAND

<table>
<tr><th>FROM</th><th>AT</th><th colspan="2">RETURN FARES (Third Class)</th></tr>
<tr><td></td><td>a.m.</td><td>s.</td><td>d.</td></tr>
<tr><td>Abergavenny (B. Rd.) ... ...</td><td>6 55</td><td rowspan="6">4</td><td rowspan="6">0</td></tr>
<tr><td>Govilon ... ...</td><td>7 0</td></tr>
<tr><td>Gilwern Halt A ... ...</td><td>7 5</td></tr>
<tr><td>Clydach Halt A ... ...</td><td>7 10</td></tr>
<tr><td>Gelli Felen Halt B ... ...</td><td>7 15</td></tr>
<tr><td>Brynmawr ... ...</td><td>7 25</td></tr>
<tr><td>Beaufort ... ...</td><td>7 35</td><td rowspan="5">3</td><td rowspan="5">6</td></tr>
<tr><td>Nantybwch ... ...</td><td>7 40</td></tr>
<tr><td>Sirhowy ... ...</td><td>7 45</td></tr>
<tr><td>Tredegar ... ...</td><td>7 50</td></tr>
<tr><td>Bedwellty Pits C ... ...</td><td>8 0</td></tr>
<tr><td>Holly Bush ... ...</td><td>8 5</td><td rowspan="4">3</td><td rowspan="4">0</td></tr>
<tr><td>Markham Village Halt D ... ...</td><td>8 10</td></tr>
<tr><td>Argoed ... ...</td><td>8 15</td></tr>
<tr><td>Blackwood ... ...</td><td>8 25</td></tr>
<tr><td>Pontllanfraith ... ...</td><td>8 30</td><td>2</td><td>6</td></tr>
<tr><td></td><td>a.m.</td><td></td><td></td></tr>
<tr><td>Barry Island ... ... arr.</td><td>9 51</td><td></td><td></td></tr>
</table>

NOTE.—This amended announcement cancels handbill O 1403/R

A—Tickets must be obtained in advance from Govilon.
B— " " " " " " " Brynmawr.
C— " " " " " " " Tredegar or Holly Bush.
D— " " " " " " between 8-30 a.m. and 6-0 p.m.

RETURN ARRANGEMENTS

Passengers return same day, leaving Barry Island at 8-0 p.m.

Children under 3 years of age, free; 3 and under 14, half-fares.

CONDITIONS OF ISSUE OF EXCURSION AND OTHER TICKETS AT LESS THAN ORDINARY FARES.

These Tickets are issued subject to the Notices and Conditions shown in the Company's current Time Tables. For luggage allowances also see Time Tables.

Further particulars and tickets in advance may be obtained at the Stations and Agencies.

All information regarding cheap travel and other facilities on the London, Midland Scottish Railway will be supplied on application to the Stations, Agencies, or Mr. C. H. TAIT, District Goods and Passenger Manager, Victoria Station, SWANSEA. (Telephone 2161, Extension 14.)

August, 1936.
(E.R.O. 53302)

ASHTON DAVIES,
Chief Commercial Manager.

Pontllanfraith (Low Level) GWR, looking towards Crumlin. *Author's Collection*

Penar Junction with the Pontypool Road line running to the left and Hall's Road to the right. *R.H. Marrows*

Penar Junction signal box. Hall's Road crosses the main line at an angle just beyond the signal box. The home signal to Penar Junction leads (*left*) to Pontypool Road and (*right*) to Hall's Road and tunnel. *R.H. Marrows*

Penar tunnel, west end on a gradient of 1 in 73. *Author's Collection*

Pantyresk automatic crossing, on the lower section of Hall's Road between Penar Junction and Hall's Road Junction. *Author's Collection*

Rock Inn, situated between Argoed and Blackwood. This was an important place (in the early years) and used for Council meetings and Petty sessions for the Bedwellty District.
Courtesy Cyril Jones

Cwrtybella church near Oakdale. The level crossing was on the Hall's Road (GWR) line. All has disappeared (including the Church and cottages) except for the crossing keepers house. The line in the middle of the photograph was called Barnes siding.
Author's Collection

Chapter Eight

The Penllwyn Tramroad

The Penllwyn Tramroad was built for John Jones and Sir Charles Morgan, land owners in the Sirhowy Valley. John Jones had acquired by marriage the estate of Penllwynsarph near Pontllanfraith with the intention of developing some 300 acres of mineral land in the Sirhowy Valley. He engaged Thomas Wakeman, a Surveyor of Gloucester to prepare plans for the tramroad.

In 1821 Jones approached the Monmouthshire Canal Co, asking them to use powers given to them in their Act of 1792 to build tramroads up to a distance of 8 miles to act as feeders to the Canal. This they refused to do, so John Jones and his partner, Sir Charles Morgan began to construct their tramroad. Samuel Homfray and his associates (Sirhowy Tramroad Co.) were naturally alarmed at this and sought and obtained an injunction in the High Court. Fortunately, common sense prevailed, resulting in an agreement being reached by all parties concerned for the Penllwyn Tramroad to be constructed, subject to certain conditions, one of which was that the lower two miles should be vested in the Sirhowy Tramroad Company which maintained this section under an agreement of 14th February, 1824. The remainder, between Ynysddu and Blackwood, continued as private property and was known as the Llanarth Tramroad. John Jones lived at Llanarth Court, situated between Abergavenny and Raglan. Mineral traffic from the small levels in the Blackwood area was worked by horse-power to Nine Mile Point as early as 1825. The actual point of connection at Nine Mile Point was over the Sirhowy River bridge of 58 ft span on to the Monmouthshire Railway & Canal section of the Sirhowy Tramroad.

The permanent way was formed of cast iron angle plates laid on stone block sleepers to a gauge of 4 ft 2 in. with loops for passing places. Much of it ran fairly close to the Sirhowy River. The Rock & Fountain Inn at Blackwood on the track side is reputed to have been the Penllwyn's Weigh Office, and one of John Jones's employees Morgan Thomas, was brought from Mamhilad near Pontypool to act as tramroad Agent at Ynysddu, and to live at the house known as 'Tyr Agent' (Agent's House) the birthplace of the Welsh Poet 'Islwyn' (Rev'd William Thomas).

The tramway on completion was, as stated, vested in the Sirhowy Tramroad Company who agreed to maintain same, and by an Act of 1860 the Sirhowy Tramway Company became known as the Sirhowy Railway Company. By an Act dated 13th July, 1876, the Sirhowy Railway Company was vested in the LNWR Company, and on the 2 chain roll line plan of the Sirhowy Railway dated 1921, under 'Titles of Acts' the following item is shown:

> London and North Western Railway (Sirhowy Railway Vesting Act 13th July, 1876).
>
> (Including Penllwyn and Bryn Tramways).

Subsequent to 1876 it is not known what traffic, if any, was worked over the Penllwyn Tramway, until 1887 when instructions were given that a wagon was to be passed over the Tramway every year to maintain the railway company's 'Rights' and this practice was in operation until 1903, when it was considered no longer necessary.

About 1900 Burnyeat Brown decided to sink a new Pit (Coronation Colliery) near Nine Mile Point, and the LNWR agreed to relay part of the old tramroad and to provide a new connection with the Sirhowy Line, which was completed, together with a new river bridge and Nine Mile Point No. 1 Box on 16th March, 1908. There were also small goods depots provided at Wattsville (1913), Cwmfelinfach (1911), and Ynysddu (Lower) (1911) which came under the supervision of the Ynysddu station master. The village of Wattsville was named after E.H. Watts, Chairman of the United National Collieries Ltd. The portion of line over the river bridge at Nine Mile Point to Wattsville Goods was removed in 1914, consequently, this depot, which closed on 2nd August, 1929, could only be reached by the new connection and a back shunt. Ynysddu Goods Depot was the larger of the three, with goods shed, offices, stables and a crane and was opened in July 1911 and closed on 1st December, 1937, the track being removed in September 1940 leaving just 1 mile in place. Much of the material for the building of Ynysddu, Cwmfelinfach, and Wattsville came over the Tramroad.

The Llanarth section (Ynysddu–Blackwood) was worked entirely by horses and was in use for only about 40 years.

A letter from the District Engineer, Abergavenny in 1937 gives much information on the Tramway in the 20th century and is worth quoting extensively:

> In 1900 Messrs Burnyeat Brown and Company (Proprietors of the Abergorky Collieries) Treorchy, near Pontypridd first proposed sinking a pit for coal adjacent to the Penllwyn Tramroad, and in July, 1902, this work was put in hand, where the Nine Mile Point Colliery exists today. Previous to the sinking of the pit, however, a proposal was in correspondence to provide a new connecting line between the Sirhowy Railway (between 14¾ and 15 m.p.) and the Penllwyn Tramway to deal with the traffic from the new Colliery, the scheme being approved by the L&NW Directors in 1902, when an Agreement was entered into between Messrs Burnyeat Brown and Company and the LNW Coy. dated 22nd May, 1902, whereby the Railway Company undertook the construction of the double junction and sidings, &c. with their Sirhowy Line, a Junction with the Penllwyn Tramway and the taking up of a portion of the existing Tramway and relaying same.
>
> By this Agreement the Colliery Company were authorised to construct an embankment across the Sirhowy Valley and a bridge across the Sirhowy River, together with a connecting line and sidings between the junctions mentioned above, which were being laid by the Railway Company. In addition the Colliery Company were authorised to take up and relay the Penllwyn Tramway between their Colliery and Nine Mile Point, the whole of the cost of the work (including the cost of the Railway Company's work) to be borne by the Colliery Company. Under Clause 10 of this Agreement the Colliery Company were empowered to work their traffic over the relaid portion of the Penllwyn Tramway between the Colliery and Nine Mile Point, by means of their own private engines, this privilege was however to cease on the completion of the new connecting line, and the traffic was thereafter to be worked over the new line.
>
> A supplemental Agreement was entered into between the Railway Company and

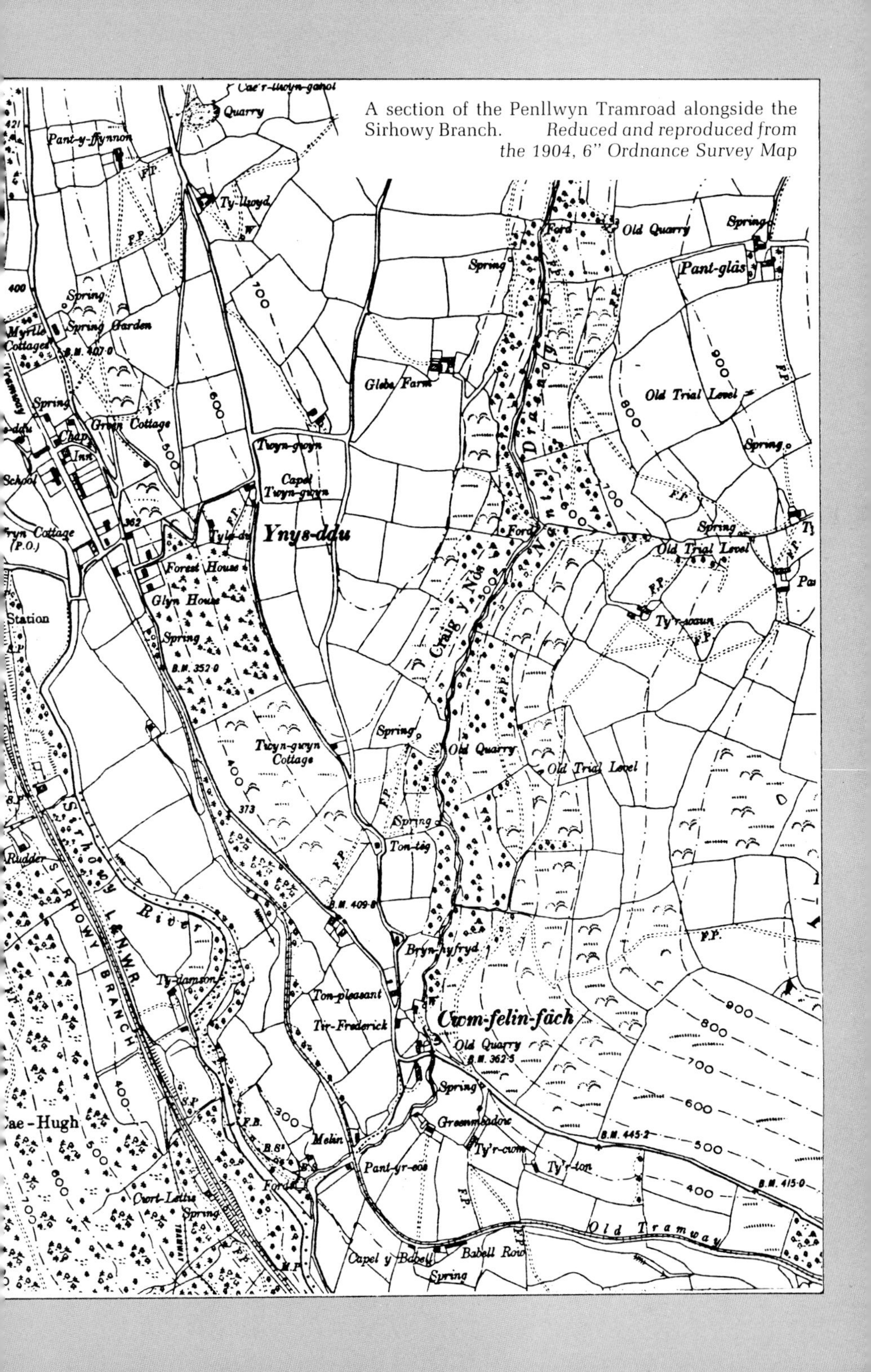

A section of the Penllwyn Tramroad alongside the Sirhowy Branch. *Reduced and reproduced from the 1904, 6" Ordnance Survey Map*

Messrs Burnyeat Brown and Company dated 12th June, 1903, whereby the Railway Company took up and relaid a further short length of the Penllwyn Tramway at the Colliery Company's expense and the Colliery Company were authorised to raise the level of a length of the Tramway adjacent to, and to the West of their colliery.

The materials for the relaying of the Tramway done by the Colliery Company were supplied them by the L&NW Railway Company.

Owing to the heavy toll the Great Western Railway Company enacted for all traffic coming off the Penllwyn Tramway which had to pass over their siding connection at Nine Mile Point Station, a proposal was put forward in 1903–4 that an independent connection should be provided from off the L&NW Company's Line at this place, the GWR connection to be removed, and an order was issued for the work to be put in hand. The Great Western Railway Company however, threatened to obtain an injunction to prevent their connection being removed, and the work was postponed, the work of laying the connection to the Tramroad from off the LNW Coy's line at Nine Mile Point eventually being carried out in April 1904 without interfering with the Great Western Railway Company's Line.

In 1905 the Penllwyn Tramway was relaid by the Railway Company from near Messrs Burnyeat Brown and Coy's pits to Ynysddu (Lower) under an arrangement with the Promoters of the Nine Mile Point Railway Bill, by which the Bill was withdrawn, and an Agreement was entered into with the Promoters, dated 2nd June, 1905 by which the Railway Company undertook the construction of the bridge crossing the Sirhowy River, and necessary connecting line.

There is not a copy of the Agreement dated 2nd June, 1905 in this Office, but under this document the LNW Company permit the Great Western Railway Company to send their engines, wagons &c., over the Sirhowy Railway and the siding between Messrs Burnyeat Brown and Coy's Pits, and give them the use of the sidings, etc. connected therewith.

In 1905 also a question was in hand of the possibility of running of Motor Rail Cars over the Penllwyn Tramway and the provision of Halts, but this did not materialise, and the Penllwyn Railway Act 1906* (to incorporate the Penllwyn Railway Company and for other purposes) which includes the construction of the new connection line, previously mentioned, states that the Company would not be required to carry passengers.

I understand that under the terms of the Agreement dated 2nd June, 1905 the cost of the work of relaying the Penllwyn Tramway and the provision of portion of the embankment for the Penllwyn Tramway Junction Line, carried out by Messrs Burnyeat Brown and Company, was to be refunded to the firm by the LNW Company.

The work of constructing the Penllwyn Tramway Junction Line, i.e. the bridge over the Sirhowy River and the connecting line between the Sirhowy Railway (between 14¾ and 15 mile posts) and the Penllwyn Tramway, was put in hand in 1906, and was completed in 1908 being passed by the Board of Trade Inspector in May of that year. This new Branch Line was opened for traffic in June 1908.

*The Penllwyn Railway Company was incorporated by Act of 20th July, 1906 (6 Edw. VII, cap. 70). Authorised mileage: 2 miles, 2 furlongs, 7 chains, from a junction with the Penllwyn Tramroad of the London & North Western Railway Company, being in substitution for the portion of this tramroad north of the junction near Ynysddu belonging to Viscount Tredegar and Colonel Herbert, who agreed to transfer to the company their rights for £20,000 in fully-paid ordinary shares. It was intended to develop the mineral resources on the east side of the Sirhowy Valley. Period for completion, five years.

An Act of 1911 extended the time for completion to 20th July, 1914; but no portion of the proposed line north of Ynysddu was ever built and an Act of 20th May, 1920 (10 & 11 Geo. cap. 13) provided for the winding-up of the company.

In 1906 a loop siding was laid in at Cwmfelinfach on the relaid tramway about half a mile from Ynysddu (Lower) and in 1908 this loop line was extended.

A new Goods Yard and sidings were provided by the Railway Company at Ynysddu (Lower) in 1911, the work being completed in July 1911, and another Goods Depot, i.e. cart road and two sidings, was constructed near the Dyffryn Farm (between the Colliery and Nine Mile Point Station) the work being authorised by Goods Traffic Minute No. 9710 15.2.11, and called the 'Wattsville Goods Depot'. This accommodation was provided for Station to Station traffic (not requiring covering) but as the traffic which it was hoped, when the accommodation was provided, would be dealt with at Wattsville Depot, did not materialise, the two sidings were taken up and removed in 1929.

The connections to the old Penllwyn Tramway at Nine Mile Point, which existed previous to the construction of the new connecting Junction line in 1906 –8 i.e. the original connection between the old Tramroad and the Monmouthshire Company's line (now GWR) and the connection from the L&NW Company's Sirhowy Line, laid in 1904 were taken up and removed in 1914 and the portion of the tramway between Nine Mile Point and Wattsville Yard was removed about the same time.

Complaints were made in 1919 by the Tredegar Goods Guards of the restricted space for working between the line and the hedge on the south side of the Penllwyn Tramway between the colliery and Wattsville, and meetings took place between the various Departments and the Colliery Company, and I would refer you to Goods Traffic Committee Minute No. 13,319 dated 15.10.19 respecting the proposal to allow Messrs Burnyeat Brown and Company to tip refuse for filling up the land on the south side of the line. A draft Agreement was prepared in 1920, but so far as I am aware this was not completed. A connection was put in by the Railway Company in 1920, apparently for a proposed tip siding, this connection is in existence to-day, but the siding was never laid in.

In 1920 the Penllwyn Railway (Abandonment) Act was passed 'for the Abandonment of the Undertaking and Winding-up and Dissolution of the Penllwyn Railway Company and for matters incidental thereto.'

The foregoing is the History of the Tramway as far as I am in a position to supply it, and no premises or works, other than the United National Collieries, Nine Mile Point, are connected with the Tramway, but I understand the Traffic Department work traffic over the Branch to Ynysddu Lower once or twice a week.

An extract from *The South Wales Argus* for 28th January, 1930 seems appropriate here:

Ebenezer Williams says – There was a tramway to Blackwood and I remember the Welsh Poet 'Islwyn' and Mrs Thomas setting out on a journey with Edward Edwards driving the pony 'Jack' and I also remember the opening of the railway station and the stopping of the first train here at Ynysddu 65 years ago – Mr Williams says it was August 25 or 27, 1865. Up to that date trains of the old Sirhowy Railway stopped at the Tredegar Arms, Pontllanfraith, where there was no platform. Then a station was built at Ynysddu – it boasted a platform and a Station Master, Mr Stephen Morgan. The train of three little black coaches, with a chocolate coloured engine, puffed in, and I remember that the driver was George Price, and that William Oliver was the guard. The coaches had hard seats. Mr Williams was a stone-cutter by trade, but had spent many years in railway work and was an LNW man in 1870 at Pontllanfraith when Mr David Owen was the Station Master.

LNWR 'Coal' tank No. 7834 at Gaer Junction with a Tredegar–Newport train at an unknown date, but probably immediately post-War. Note the ex-Lancashire and Yorkshire coach bringing up the rear. *John Hodge Collection*

Ivatt 2–6–2T No. 41203 on Risca Viaduct with a train from Newport in the early 1950s; these locomotives replaced the 'Coal' tanks. A down mineral train from Nine Mile Point is just visible on the opposite line. *John Hodge*

Appendix One

Hall's Road – a Brief Survey

Hall's Road was owned and built by Benjamin Hall, son-in-law of Richard Crawshay, the Cyfarthfa Ironmaster. Hall was the father of Sir Benjamin Hall, later Lord Llanover, who as chief Commissioner of Works was responsible for the clock on the Tower of the Houses of Parliament, known universally as 'Big Ben'. Hall's Road was built piece-meal between 1805 and 1814 and led from the Monmouthshire Western Valley Tramroad above Risca, running parallel with the Ebbw River and Monmouthshire Canal for nearly three miles to Abercarn and then turning sharply westward to Pentwynmawr and into the Sirhowy Valley, terminating originally in the Manmoel area. When the Tredegar Iron & Coal Company sunk Markham Colliery in 1912, the line was extended to this point.

It seems the Tramroad was completed as far as the Waterloo Colliery at the Gwrhay, near Argoed by 1811 and the remainder to the Manmoel area by 1814. Sir Henry Prothero, of Malpas Court, Newport, Thomas Phillips, Barrister, (later to become Mayor of Newport in 1839) and the Barnes Family were all very early and active proprietors in the district.

Hall died in July 1817, but before this he let a colliery in 1815 to Evan and Lewis Lewis, and to three other partners; one was Zephaniah Williams, the Chartist Leader, who lived for a time in the Gwrhay area of Argoed. During the transitional period and conversion from plateway to railway, all standard waggons were fitted with special wheels devised by Summers Harford, Ebbw Vale Works to run on either 4 ft 2 in. plateway or standard gauge edge-rails. Hall's Road was laid with edge-rails to railway standard by 30th September, 1860.

Collieries using Hall's Tramroad all lay north of Newbridge and it is probable that once the Taff Vale Extension from Pontypool to the Sirhowy Valley had been completed, coal was transferred to that line at Pentwynmawr where the railway crossed the Tramroad on the level, leaving the tramroad down through the tunnel to Hall's Road Junction in the Western Valley unused for a time.

The Taff Vale Extension formed junctions in the early 1860s at two points with the Sirhowy Railway at Pontllanfraith forming a triangle and from 1865 the GW coal traffic from the Taff Valley intended for Newport went via Pontllanfraith and down the Sirhowy branch, which became LNWR property in 1875. Relations at this time between the LNW and GW were not good and the former withdrew the GW running powers from Sirhowy Junction to Nine Mile Point. To obtain a shorter route to Newport the GW leased for a 1000 years Hall's Tramroad from Baroness Llanover with the intention of converting it into a railway, but in the meantime an agreement was reached with the LNW, which enabled the GW to resume running its through coal trains between Tredegar Junction Lower and Nine Mile Point as from 1st February, 1877. Later, the LNW granted permanent running powers. GW passenger trains, including excursion traffic from the Aberdare direction, used this route at times.

The 3¾ miles between Penar Junction on the Taff Vale Extension line and Manmoel Colliery was opened as a standard gauge railway on 10th March, 1886. The southern section, which involved re-alignment and the enlarging of Penar Tunnel to take steam locomotives, was not similarly dealt with until September 1912.

On 20th November, 1967 the southern part of Hall's Road was closed and the coal traffic from Markham and Oakdale collieries was brought down to Penar Junction and reversed to Pontllanfraith and the Sirhowy line via Nine Mile Point. It reverted back to the full length of Hall's Road on 2nd May, 1970 when the lower section of the Sirhowy Branch closed. The line was single from Hall's Road Junction to Penar Junction, double from Penar Junction to Colliers Arms, and single again up over Court-y-bella Crossing to Markham Colliery. The double line section Penar Junction–Colliers Arms was made in the period 1912–15 during the sinking of Markham Colliery and further development of Oakdale Colliery.

The section between Hall's Road Junction and Penar Junction was worked by Electric Train Token, and from Colliers Arms to Markham Colliery by Wooden Train Staff coloured Red. Markham Colliery closed in 1986 and Oakdale in 1989; the Hall's Road branch is now closed. The GWR locomotives in use were the 2–8–0 tank engines of the '42XX' and '52XX' classes and the 2–8–2 tanks of the converted '72XX' class. The Panniers were occasionally seen but rarely ran beyond Colliers Arms. Later, in 1959, class '9F' 2–10–0 No. 92166, with the Barkley Mechanical Stoker System was seen working for a few months. Class 37 diesels continued to be used until closure.

Although the Hall's Road branch was essentially a mineral line, taking coal from all the collieries from Markham right down to Tyr-Philkins at one time, many will be surprised to learn that as from 14th March, 1927, a passenger service (auto-train) ran from Oakdale and Penmaen Halts to Pontypool Road, some trains returning from Crumlin H.L. Oakdale Halt closed on 12th September, 1932 and the service ceased from Penmaen Halt on 25th September, 1939.

Viaduct carrying Hall's Road across a dingle at Abernant-y-Felin between Argoed and Markham. The viaduct was later filled in because of subsidence. *Author's Collection*

Appendix Two

Collieries Served by the Valley's Railways

(With thanks to R.A. Cooke for additional information)

The Tredegar Iron & Coal Company was formed in 1873 to take over the enterprise started in 1800 by Samuel Homfray, Richard Fothergill, and Matthew Monkhouse, the founders of the Tredegar Iron Works. Listed below are the names involved in the development of the company:

Isaac Lowthian Bell
William Menelaus
Henry Davis Pochin
William Newmarch
Sydney Carr Glyn
Benjamin Whitworth
Edward Williams
James Wyllie
Charles & Arthur Markham

All the collieries detailed had connections at one time with the Sirhowy Branch or Hall's Road (GWR). The Steam Coal Pits were owned by the Tredegar Iron & Coal Company except Coronation Colliery at Nine Mile Point worked by Burnyeat Brown Ltd. The last to close was Oakdale Colliery in 1989. Markham and Wyllie were all-electric when built. Oakdale switched to electricity sometime after the last war. Four of the Tredegar Iron & Coal Company's Collieries were named after Directors, such as Whitworth, Pochin, Markham and Wyllie. Abernant and Llanover Collieries, of the Bargoed Coal Company were sunk near a beauty spot in the valley, the bridge over the Sirhowy river called Pont Abernant-y-felin. The land in the area was the subject of much dispute with regard to ownership between Lady Llanover, the Revd J.M. Traherne, Sir Henry Prothero, and others. The site was even considered at one stage for a Gun Powder Factory! Llanover Colliery takes its name from the Llanover Estate; all its traffic going over Hall's Road. Hollybush and Oakdale were named after the woods in the district, Bedwellty Pits Colliery from the Parish of that name. Ty Trist (House of Sadness) was so known because of major setbacks in its early development. There was usually a good relationship between the railway company and local colliery management for the clearance of traffic.

List of Collieries

(In order from top of Valley down)

Navigation Colliery, Graham Bros & Co.

Colliery	Owner
Whitworth Colliery	Tredegar Iron & Coal Co.
Ty Trist Colliery	
Bedwellty Colliery	
Pochin Colliery	

Hollybush Colliery, E.D. Williams.
Abernant Colliery, Bargoed Coal Company.
Llanover Colliery, Bargoed Coal Company.
Rhoswen Colliery, Bevan & Pryce.
Cwm Creeich Colliery, Various Owners.
Rock & Primrose, Various Owners.

Markham Colliery pithead, Hall's Road (GWR). *Author*

Upper Cwm Gelly, Gelli Dywylt Coal Co. 1817.
Lower Cwm Gelly, Budd & Co.
Rock or New Rock Colliery, Various Owners.
Libanus Siding, Matthews.
Wyllie Colliery.
Lord Tredegar's Siding, Wentlodge Colliery & Brick Works (1879). Later – Christopher Pond.
Coronation Colliery, Nine Mile Point, Burnyeat Brown Ltd.
Rock Vein Colliery.
Black Vein Colliery.
Sun Vein or Risca Colliery.

Hall's Road

Markham Colliery, Markham Heam Coal Co.
Manmoel Colliery, C. Pond.
Llanover Colliery, Various Owners.
Twyn Simon Colliery, Bowditch Bros.
Gwrhay (Islwyn) Colliery, Various Owners.
Waterloo Colliery, Various Owners.
Penrhin Colliery, Various Owners.
Oakdale Colliery, Oakdale Navigation Collieries Ltd.
Woodford Colliery, Various Owners.
Tir Philkins (Kincoed) Colliery, Various Owners.
Twyn Gwyn, Twyn Gwyn Colliery Co (on lower section).

Sirhowy Valley Collieries

Depth and Size of Colliery Shafts

Name	*Depth*	*Size*
Whitworth No. 1	315 ft	–
Whitworth No. 2	558 ft	–
Ty Trist No. 1	651 ft	15 ft × 10 ft
Ty Trist No. 2	414 ft	–
Bedwellty No. 1	831 ft	–
Bedwellty No. 2	699 ft	–
Pochin North	1347 ft	18 ft dia.
Pochin South	1347 ft	16 ft dia.
Hollybush	100 ft	–
Markham North	1845 ft	–
Markham South	1851 ft	–
Abernant West	489 ft	16 ft × 10 ft
Abernant East	495 ft	16 ft × 11 ft
Llanover	551 ft	15 ft dia.
Oakdale South	2085 ft	21 ft dia.
Oakdale North	2187 ft	21 ft dia.
Wyllie North	1788 ft	–
Wyllie South	1896 ft	–
Nine Mile Point West	1177 ft	–
Nine Mile Point East	1151 ft	–

(Size of shaft not known in all cases.)

An extract from the *South Wales Argus* for 22nd April, 1907 shows the elaborate arrangements made by the railway companies for the running of special trains for the cutting of the first sod at Oakdale Colliery – even going to the trouble of making temporary platforms, there being no stations at these places. The Great Western Railway reaped the benefit later; not only at Oakdale, but at Llanover and Markham when they were sunk. This was indeed a chance to celebrate and these Welsh communities certainly made the most of it!

Cutting of the first sod by Mrs Markham (*see page 65*)

Naturally the cutting of the first sod of the new sinkings was made the most of locally. Argoed Village was *en féte*; and there was a liberal display of flags and bunting. The little Village of Gwrhay, nestling under the mountain on the other side of the hill looked more sombre from a distance but upon getting to the place all was life and activity. All were picturing the future when the snorts of the winding engine would herald the winning of the coal; when the quiet hillside village would become a busy thriving town; and when the pretty corner of the valley would be spoilt by unsightly tips. Rhiw-syr-dafydd people, who live on the other side of the colliery, were equally as curious and could hardly imagine so many people in their neighbourhood. The directors made elaborate arrangements to celebrate the event. A representative company of guests were invited, and although many found themselves unable to accept on account of other engagements, there was a large attendance. They travelled in special trains; the London & North Western Company running a fine saloon train from Abergavenny for the benefit of the Sirhowy Valley passengers as far as the Rock; while the Great Western ran a special from Cardiff and Newport; which travelled on the Penar Branch to the site of the new sinkings. Beyond the particular event of the day, the presence of a passenger train, especially with the splendid accommodation afforded for travelling by the Great Western on this branch was a novelty in itself and further emphasised the importance the district had suddenly assumed. Its progress along the valley was watched with considerable interest and excitement among the large crowd which lined the mountainside overlooking the site of the sinkings when its approach was announced. As it steamed up to the improvised platform a volley of detonators echoed through the valley as an indication that the train had reached its destination. The guests lost no time in proceeding to the site.

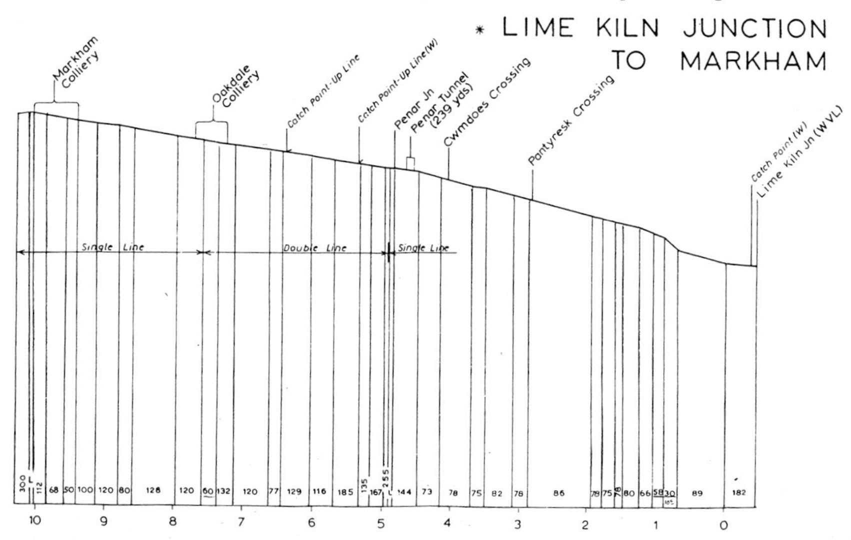

Appendix Three

A List of Station Masters

Nantybwch

J. Kevenagh
R. O'Connor
J. Stedman

Sirhowy

H. Duck
I. White
A. Hodder
J. Wiliams

Tredegar

J. Hutchings
A. Harry
H. Diggory
J. Thomas
T. Harries
A. Price
G. Davies

Bedwellty Pits

W. Davies
C. Carter
A. Humphries

Hollybush

D. Williams
F. Siford
W. Owen
W. Edwards
F. Davies
H. Leadbeater
E. Edwards
C. Jones
Jones

Markham Village

J. Lewis
T. Tasker

Argoed

Robert Howell
Evan Lones
Frank Reynolds
E. Edwards
W. Morgan

Blackwood

Cornelius Bohane
T. Harris
H.W. Forrester
J. Restall
W.J. Michael
L. Lloyd

Pontllanfraith

D. Owen
T. Childes
William Matthews
J. Griffiths
– Eccleston
S. Davies
W. Hill
– Bentley
W. Summerhill

Ynysddu

Stephen Morgan
William Morgan
E. Jones
J. Williams
F. O'Connor
H. Davies
E. Rees
L. Lloyd

Pont Lawrence

H. Lewis
H. Leadbeater
W. Edwards
G. Morgan

Nine Mile Point

W.H. Francis
A.T. Robinson
S. Morgan
W. Owen
H. Davies
W. Phillips
L. Lloyd
A.G. Ray

NOTE: The list is not able to be described as 'complete'.

Blackwood station showing wooden extensions to each platform which were originally staggered. *Lens of Sutton*

Bibliography

The Sirhowy Valley and its Railways. D.S. Barrie and Charles E. Lee.
Reflections on a Railway Career. J.M. Dunn.
The Railway Magazine September 1911. The Monmouthshire Railway. Herbert Rake.
The Railway Magazine July 1960. The Railways of Newport. William J. Skillern, FLA.
The Locomotive Magazine January 15, 1915.
The Locomotive Magazine February 15, 1915.
Slaters Royal Directory of Herefordshire, Monmouthshire, 1850.
Lascelles & Co., *Directory & Gazettier*, County of Monmouth, 1852.
Morris & Co., *Commercial Directory*, Counties of Hereford and Monmouth, 1862.
Kellys Directory of South Wales & Monmouthshire, 1895.
Kellys Directory of South Wales & Monmouthshire, 1910.
The Welsh Coal & Shipping Hand Book, 1916.
Diaries of Gwillim Jenkins, Mason, 1867–1878.
My Father's Diaries, 1888–1919.